The Knights Templar & Hospitaller in Herefordshire

The Knights Templar & Hospitaller in Herefordshire

by

Audrey Tapper

Logaston Press

LOGASTON PRESS
Little Logaston Woonton Almeley
Herefordshire HR3 6QH
logastonpress.co.uk

First published by Logaston Press 2005
Reprinted 2006, 2009

ISBN 978 1904396 35 2

Typeset by Logaston Press
and printed in Great Britain by
Bell & Bain Ltd., Glasgow

Contents

Acknowledgements

My thanks to all the people I have contacted in Herefordshire and further afield who have been so generous with their time and information. In particular I would like to thank the staff of English Heritage, Gloucester Record Office, Gwent Record Office, Hereford Reference Library, Herefordshire Sites and Monuments Record, Hereford Record Office, Monmouth Library, and Shropshire Records and Research Centre with whom I have been in contact. Those whom I would like to thank by name include Vernon Amor of the Wye Valley Brewery, Ingram Barrell of Garway, Stephen Clarke of Monmouth Archaeological Society, Professor C.C. Dyer, Carolyn and John Eaton of Garway, Professor Peter Edbury, Sally Gale, Les Good, Mary Hopson of Llanrothal, Sue Hubbard, Dave Jemmett of Monmouth Archaeological Society, Mary Jones of Bosbury, Hazel Lewis of the St. John's Ambulance Brigade in Wales, Carl F. Nicholson, Kate Orr, Richard Pearce of the Golden Crust Bakery Ross-on-Wye, A.L. Sockett of Monmouth Archaeological Society, Rosemarie and Michael Sparey of Garway, David Walker, and Pamela Willis of the Museum and Library of the Order of St. John at Clerkenwell. I am especially grateful to my husband and son for their invaluable help and support, and to Andy Johnson of Logaston Press whose encouragement and expertise have brought this project to fruition.

For use of illustrations I acknowledge the following: John Tapper for those on pages 47, 54, 59, 61, 64, 66, 68 and 69; Logaston Press for those on pages 5 and 6; Essex County Council for that on page 23; Malcolm Thurlby for those on pages 44 and 45; University of Cambridge Air Photo Library for that on page 49; Danny West for that on pages 50-51 and Archaeological Investigations for that on page 62.

Introduction

I wonder if my interest in the Knights of the Temple and the Hospital would have developed in the way it did if we had not come to live in Garway, when my husband was appointed headteacher of the primary school there. I still remember the first visit to St. Michael's Church, its wonderful simplicity and serenity giving a sense of peace that for me has never diminished.

It was many years later that Sue Hubbard organised evening sessions at Hereford Record Office and I, like many others who were not free during the day, took the opportunity to discover more about our local history. I imagined that I would soon find out everything about the church and all the people who had lived in the village since it had been built. What I did find out very quickly was that it isn't that easy. However, with lots of help from Sue and the HRO I began to gather information and like everyone else who is interested in local history became sidetracked at every step. In the end my interest became focused on the Knights Templar and Hospitaller who had in turn owned the estate at Garway.

This booklet is about those Knights and the properties they were given in Herefordshire. The information I have gathered varies from detailed information such as Beatrice Lees' *Records of the Knights Templar in the 12th Century* and Rev. Larking's edited account of the 1338 report of the Hospitaller properties in England, to the especially interesting local work carried out by professionals and amateurs which has been recorded in the Woolhope Transactions. Larking's own publication was the result of initial misfortune, for he was 'compelled by ill-health to pass the winter of 1838–1839 in the island of Malta and took the opportunity to inspect the MSs in the Public Library at Valletta', where he found the information for his report.

All the Templar and Hospitaller properties in Herefordshire have their place in the history of the county but it is only at Garway that tangible evidence can be found proving that both Orders occupied the estate there. The church, tower and dovecote are a wonderful inheritance and enduring examples of the workmanship of the medieval builders. But such buildings are expensive to maintain, and sales of this booklet through St. Michael's Church will help raise funds to preserve its fabric.

Conquerors, Pilgrims and Crusaders

In 1066 William the Conqueror arrived in England and as he and his victorious army made rapid progress through the newly acquired country, he rewarded the men who had supported him in the enterprise. From these grateful barons, knights and bishops, William expected complete allegiance and the appropriate knights' fees. Knights' fees, the number specified by the king in each case, were designed to ensure that fully equipped knights accompanied by their grooms and servants would be ready to join the king's army at a moment's notice.

When William and his army reached the Welsh border their progress was hampered, like that of the Roman Legions a thousand years earlier, by the natural barrier of the Welsh hills. The Romans had set up three strategically positioned Legionary Fortresses in the Welsh Marches—*Deva* in the north, *Viroconium* in the centre and *Isca* in the south, now known as Chester, Wroxeter and Caerleon. King William followed almost the same line of defence by setting up three of his most trusted men in Earldoms along the border at Chester, Shrewsbury and Hereford, thus securing the north, central and southern Marches and containing the Welsh in the west. He did not have time for the slow penetration and conquest of Wales so his solution to the problem was the creation of Marcher Lords. These wealthy and powerful men had already been given important English estates and now they were given free rein in the Welsh Marches. Their only loyalty was to the king and they were allowed supreme judicial authority in all the Welsh land they could take and hold. In England in subsequent years castles could not be raised without the king's licence to crenellate but the Marcher Lords had no such restriction, their power in their own land was absolute.

Once a Norman lord had an area safely under control, with his earth and timber and in subsequent years stone castle dominating the newly subjugated territory, it was the usual procedure for him to found a monastery. The medieval expectation of the after life was clear, those who had led pure lives would exist happily in Heaven while the sinful would suffer purgatory forever. The line between good and evil was often hazy and it wasn't always easy to be pure, but the church had the answer and there were ways to atone for any 'mistakes'. The Norman invaders knew the cost in lives that they had incurred in the conquest and maybe saw the gift of monasteries and land as a way to pave their path away from hell. Whatever the reason, monasteries sprang up throughout the newly conquered land, often in the shadow of the castle walls, as daughter houses to the monasteries that the Norman Lords had associations with in their homeland. William Fitz Osbern, Earl of Hereford, gave land in Chepstow for a priory, Hamelin de Ballon, Lord of Abergavenny, endowed the Priory of St. Mary, Gwethenoc, Lord of Monmouth founded Monmouth Priory—the list goes on and on.

Just 30 years after William of Normandy's successful conquest of England, Pope Urban II resolved to free the Holy City of Jerusalem from the Turks and bring Jerusalem under the protection of Rome.

Jerusalem had always been a place of pilgrimage for the Jewish people and it was there that Jesus had been celebrating the Jewish Feast of the Passover when he was arrested, tried and put to death. Early in the 4th century, in the night before the crucial battle of Milvian Bridge near Rome, the Roman Emperor Constantine had a dream in which he saw a cross on the sun. Taking this as an omen he told his soldiers to paint the Christian monogram *Chi Rho*, the first two letters of the Greek word for Christ, on their shields. Constantine won the battle and immediately became converted, believing that the Christians' God had intervened to give him victory. His mother Helena became a Christian too and made a pilgrimage to the Holy Land where she has been credited with the foundation of churches. One of these was the Church of the Holy Sepulchre upon the site of Jesus's crucifixion and burial, and as a result Jerusalem also became a focus of Christian pilgrimage.

But Jerusalem soon became the centre of pilgrimage not just for Jews and Christians but also for Muslims. In 688 the city was taken by the Muslims who built the Dome of the Rock, but they had not felt threatened by the presence of Jews or Christians in Jerusalem and committed no acts of persecution, indeed the religions lived together comparatively harmoniously while steadfastly maintaining their own religious devotions. There was even an abbey, St. Mary of the Latins, which had been founded by Italian merchants of Amalfi to provide shelter for Christian pilgrims, not altogether a philanthropic gesture as much of their business was concerned with the transport of pilgrims from Italy to the Holy Land. This amicable state of affairs came to an end in 969 when Jerusalem came under Egyptian control. In 1010 the caliph ordered the destruction of the Christian shrines and in 1071 the Holy Land was lost to the Turks.

There was a tremendous response to Pope Urban's call to take up the cross, rewards in Heaven could surely be guaranteed by such acts. There were other incentives too. The method of inheritance in Europe at this time was primogeniture by which the eldest son was heir to his father's estate while his brothers and sisters had nothing. There was always the Church as a career, but few of the sons of noblemen became scholars. Most had been trained for knighthood from an early age and all over Europe many young, vigorous, eager and penniless knights were seeking a purpose. By supporting the pope's appeal not only could they secure the safety of their souls and find satisfaction in their expertise, there was also the opportunity to become wealthy. One of the advantages of battle was the taking of hostages for the ransoms in land and money they fetched.

It was agreed that the crusaders would leave in August 1096. This would give Urban time to spread the word and organise his leaders; his own personal representative was to be Bishop Adehemar of Le Puy. Once the harvest was safely in the various groups, under their local leaders, left their homes and made their way to Constantinople, some arriving late in 1096 and others early in 1097. Once the main force had assembled the men of the First Crusade were ferried across the Bosporus to continue their trek to Jerusalem.

Almost three years after setting out the crusaders reached Jerusalem and on 15th July 1099 they took the city. In the frenzied massacre that followed, men, women and children, both Muslims and Jews, were cut down. A Christian knight described the atrocity: 'Our men followed and pursued them, killing and hacking as far as the Temple of Solomon and there was such slaughter that our men were up to their ankles in blood.' Another wrote: 'If you would hear how we treated our enemies at Jerusalem, know that in the portico of Solomon and in the Temple our men rode through the unclean blood of the Saracens, which came up to the knees of our horses.'

It is possible that neither Pope Urban nor Bishop Adehemar were aware of the 'success' of their Holy Army. The bishop had died, possibly of plague, two weeks before Jerusalem was taken, and the pope just two weeks after the city fell, so maybe the news never reached him. The victorious crusader leaders were now without advice on how to govern their newly made conquests, and any instructions Adehemar may have been given had not been passed on before his own death. They therefore decided to elect a leader from amongst themselves and chose Godfrey de Bouillon. He accepted the position but refused the title 'King of Jerusalem' choosing instead to be known as 'The Defender of the Holy Sepulchre'. When he died a year later his brother had no hesitation in being crowned Baldwin I, King of Jerusalem.

The destruction of Jerusalem from the book of the Maccabees

After the successful capture of Jerusalem many of the crusaders returned home, for they had fulfilled their promise to Pope Urban and the Holy City was now safely in Christian hands. Yet Jerusalem and other lands conquered in the crusade would have to be protected, and among the knights who chose to remain were those responsible for the emergence of two of the best-known Orders of military monks—the Knights of the Hospital and the Knights of the Temple.

In Jerusalem, the Benedictine monks of the Abbey of St. Mary of the Latins offered hospitality to all pilgrims, rich and poor, Christian and non-Christian, in fact to all those who needed a haven. But for many pilgrims the arduous journey proved too much and hospitality was not enough, medical attention was necessary too. Close to the abbey a hospice was set up on the site of a church that had been dedicated to St. John the Baptist and it became known as the Hospital of St. John. It was run by a separate community of lay brothers, who were ready to devote their lives and their medical skills to care for the elderly, sick, and exhausted travellers. They too treated rich and poor alike and were often rewarded by those who could substantiate their gratitude. Some of the crusaders who had decided not to return home put away their armour and weapons and joined the Brothers of the Hospital in caring for the pilgrims in the hospice. Numbers of Christian pilgrims soon increased as freedom of access to Christian sites was now guaranteed.

Another group of crusaders decided to remain in the Holy Land to provide protection for pilgrims travelling the roads to Jerusalem and they called themselves the Poor Fellow Soldiers of Jesus Christ. Many of the pilgrims from the west made their way by land through France to Italy, then by sea to Acre and finally by road to Jerusalem. Another route was by land to Constantinople, where a ferry would take them across the Bosporus, and then a very long journey overland to Jerusalem. Both routes had plus and minus points, but added to the hazards of the journey were the constant threats of attack from pirates on sea and bandits on land. The arrival of a group of armed knights ready to escort the pilgrims on the last leg of their journey must surely have been a wonderful sight to the newly arrived travellers in the Holy Land. The knights guided the pilgrims to Jerusalem expecting no reward for keeping Christ's followers safe, but many of the pilgrims were rich and showed their gratitude for the knights' protection with generous gifts.

The Templars and Hospitallers became responsible for many castles in the Holy Land which were either given or sold to them by owners who lacked funds to maintain an adequate defence. Le Krak des Chevaliers started as such a gift in 1144 and it became the greatest and strongest of the Hospitaller castles after they had rebuilt it

The dining hall, Krak des Chevaliers

When King Baldwin I of Jerusalem died he was succeeded by his cousin, King Baldwin II, who acknowledged the work of the armed knights of the Poor Fellow Soldiers of Jesus Christ by giving them permanent accommodation in Jerusalem at the al-Aqsa Mosque, which had been built on the site of the Temple Of Solomon. On taking up residence in their new quarters they became known as 'The Poor Knights of the Temple of Solomon'.

By 1109 the Christian army had established four settlements in the Holy Land: the County of Edessa, the Principality of Antioch, the County of Tripoli and the Kingdom of Jerusalem. The crusaders knew them collectively as *Outremere*, literally their 'land beyond the sea' (the Mediterranean), and for the next two hundred years the Christian Knights of the Hospital and Temple became the standing army in the crusader states. During that time they received reinforcements when popes instigated and kings led the military expeditions known as Crusades. But in spite of their common purpose the Hospitallers and Templars were not a 'band of brothers', and there were constant disputes between the two Orders.

The Knights of the Order of St. John of Jerusalem

The tireless work of the monks of the Hospital of St. John did not go unnoticed. Godfrey de Bouillon acknowledged their work and other leaders were quick to follow his example with gifts of property or treasure. Those who had been cared for in the hospital also showed their gratitude. At this time the leader of the Hospital of St. John was Brother Gerard. He was a superb organiser and with the extra finances now available he began to extend the work begun in Jerusalem. Before long hospices had been set up all along the pilgrim routes reaching into Italy, France and Spain. The work of the brothers of the Hospital quickly became known throughout the Christian world and so impressed Pope Paschal II that in 1113 he awarded his official recognition and papal protection to the 'Order of the Hospital of St. John in Jerusalem'.

Gerard died seven years later and Raymond du Puy, one of the knights who had joined the Hospitallers after the success of the First Crusade, became Master of the Hospital in Jerusalem. Under his leadership the Hospitallers developed the military side of their Order, probably through necessity in order to help the King of Jerusalem, and became the Knights of the Hospital of St. John of Jerusalem. From the beginning the Order was made up of three groups—chaplains, knights and serving brothers. The chaplains held superior positions until 1230, when the importance of the knights was recognised and they were given precedence over the men of the church. Serving brothers fulfilled a variety of duties from sergeants-at-arms to working in the kitchens. Originally the Hospitallers wore black monastic robes over their armour but in 1259 Pope Alexander allowed them to wear a scarlet surcoat emblazoned with a simple white cross. The privilege was soon extended to all their brothers-at-arms, unlike the Templars who retained their prerogative of wearing a red cross on their white surcoats for knights only.

Even while dedicating their lives to the Holy War the Hospitallers never lost sight of their original undertaking of caring for the sick. Constantly increasing their medical expertise, they developed an excellent knowledge of drugs and herbal medicine, they understood the importance of good hygiene and the need for pure drinking water. In their superb hospitals they exercised the need to isolate infectious cases and knew the value of a calm atmosphere in the wards.[1] The Jerusalem Hospital, which had beds for 2,000 infirm of both sexes, was divided into wards with one especially for gynaecological cases, and cots were made for children who were born to women pilgrims. Four doctors and four surgeons were attached to each ward assisted by nine sergeants who washed and fed the patients, issued sheets and made beds. In 1182 a statue decreed that 2,000 sheepskins were needed, and two sick persons should share a cloak of skin, boots and a woollen cap to keep them warm when going to the latrines.

By 1302 the Christian armies had lost everything they had gained in the Holy Land since the First Crusade and both Templars and Hospitallers left to take up residence on their estates in Cyprus. But after their successful capture of Rhodes in 1310 the Hospitallers relocated there and began the fortification of their new island home. Previously all the brothers had lived together, but on Rhodes they lived as seven communities called *Langues* or tongues (languages), in separate *auberges* or inns, for Provence, Auvergne, France, Spain, Italy, England and Germany.

After the loss of the Holy Land the Hospitallers were presented with a new role. The Turks were intent on invading south-east Europe and were once again threatening Christianity. The Knights of the Hospital continued to fight, but replaced their horses with galleys. Rhodes with its excellent harbour made the perfect base and soon the Hospitallers controlled the shipping lanes of the eastern Mediterranean. When a Turkish force attacked Rhodes in 1480 the Hospitallers managed to survive three months of siege before they drove off the enemy, a victory that brought them renewed fame and a great increase in the number of recruits. In 1522 the Turks attacked again with a huge force led personally by Sultan Suliman who had great respect for the Hospitallers but was determined to take Rhodes from them. This time the siege lasted five months and finally ended when, completely out of gunpowder and ammunition and having suffered heavy casualties, the Hospitallers were forced to surrender. Impressed by the Hospitallers' heroism, Suliman allowed the survivors to leave unmolested. The Grand Master of the Order, l'Isle Adam, led his remaining knights to the harbour for their final voyage from Rhodes. The Hospitallers were now without a permanent base and dispersed throughout the Mediterranean in temporary homes provided by friends of the Order. The Grand Master spent the next four years travelling to the courts of Europe—some authorities believe he was looking for support to recapture Rhodes, others that he was looking for a new home for the Order. He was received by King Henry VIII at St. James' Palace and given guns and armour to the value of 20,000 crowns.[2]

Emperor Charles V of Spain had allowed the Hospitallers accommodation in Sicily but had grown perturbed at their long stay. Since the loss of Rhodes the Turkish naval power, unchallenged by the Hospitallers, had been able to progress further west in the Mediterranean and Charles now feared that he would soon lose his port of Tripoli on the north coast of Africa. If the Hospitallers would accept Malta and agree to defend Tripoli they would be in an excellent position to protect Christian shipping. As the Hospitallers were by this time desperate for a new home, they accepted his offer; Charles had found one solution to two problems. The guns that had been given to the Order by Henry VIII were eventually used in the defence of Tripoli. In the early 1990s one of their number was dug out from the bottom of Famagusta Harbour in Cyprus, presumably lost in transit, being identified by its two badges, one that of the Tudors and the other the coat-of-arms of l'Isle Adam.

Malta was no Rhodes but had two spacious harbours, an important fact to the Order that had become a powerful maritime force. The document drawn up makes no mention of Tripoli, but in return for the islands of Malta, Gozo and Comino, the Hospitallers were to make the Emperor a yearly presentation of a Maltese Falcon. In 1530, l'Isle Adam and his knights sailed into the Grand Harbour of Malta ready to make another new start, where the experience they had gained in fortifying Rhodes could be used to great advantage. But the problems of the Knights Hospitaller were not over.

When Pope Clement VII refused to annul Henry VIII's first marriage to Catherine of Aragon, Henry broke all ties with Rome and declared himself the Supreme Head on Earth of the Church of England. He did nothing to change the way the church was run and possibly assumed there would be no repercussion. The monastic population, however, had particularly strong links with the pope, God's deputy on earth, and queried how he could be replaced? Before a serious situation could develop Henry and his chief advisor, Thomas Cromwell, found the answer and set about removing the problem.

In 1535 they put the first phase of their plan into operation by collecting information concerning the wealth of all churches in the country. The result of the survey is known as the *Valor Ecclesiasticus* and contains details of every ecclesiastical establishment in the country from the greatest to the smallest. The following year Cromwell sent out inspectors to visit every monastic establishment in order to investigate how each was being run. Considering the number of estates involved and the distance travelled to reach them all, Thomas Cromwell and his inspectors surpassed themselves by having the report ready for Henry in the same year. The results revealed widespread corruption and extravagant lifestyles, not exactly the simple life of devotion expected of monks and nuns, but as the inspectors were working under Cromwell's direction, it was not surprising that they found just what the king was hoping for. Immediately King Henry passed the Act for the Suppression of the Lesser Monasteries, that is those with fewer than 12 monks or nuns and an income of less than £200 a year. These properties were then transferred to the Crown and the inhabitants pensioned off, with a number of the monks becoming parish priests. In 1536 the Commissioners of confiscated church lands wrote to Thomas Cromwell:

> Pleaseth it your Mastership to understand that there is a house of Black Monks called the Priory of Monmouth. I did see the said house and there is nor pot nor pan, nor bed nor bedstead, nor no monk in the said house but one, the which doth go to board in the town; and, as I am informed, the Prior is in sanctuary in Garway.

The Prior of Monmouth was safe with the Hospitallers in Garway, but not for long.

In 1537 the Act for the Suppression of the Greater Monasteries came into force and the remaining monasteries were taken over by the crown. King Henry gave some of the estates to his favourites and sold off everything else that he could, including furnishings, livestock, masonry, lead from the roofs, and the metal recovered from bells that had been melted down.

In many towns and villages, people had worshipped in the nave of the local monastic church, but with the Dissolution of the Monasteries the churches were declared redundant along with the rest of the monastic buildings. Worship played a significant part in the lives of the people and the loss of these buildings, in which they took part in the ritual that would save them from purgatory, must have been traumatic. Thus in many cases the monastic churches were purchased by the local people and there was no break in the services of Mass, Baptism, Marriage and Death, the only difference being that the monastic church was now the parish church. In Tewkesbury where almost all the monastic buildings were destroyed the townspeople who had always worshipped in the nave of the Abbey Church, purchased the whole building for £453. This was the estimated value of the bells and the lead from the roof. One of Cromwell's inspectors in Wales was Sir John Price. As the two men were related by marriage it is not really surprising to learn that Sir John was granted the Benedictine Abbey in Brecon which not only survived, but eventually in 1923 was elevated to become Brecon Cathedral.

In 1540, only 14 years after receiving and supporting l'Isle d'Adam, Grand Master of the Order, Henry VIII finally turned on the Knights of the Hospital. The Order of St. John of Jerusalem in England was abolished and members of the Order fled to Malta where English recruits continued to be accepted.

Detail from a map of the siege of Malta published in 1565

King Henry VIII died in 1547 and his son, who was only nine years old, became King Edward VI of England. Almost immediately the Catholic Religion was abandoned and England became a Protestant country. Edward died in 1553 after only six years as king and was succeeded by his half-sister Mary. Queen Mary was determined to bring the country back to the Catholic Faith and this included the re-establishment of the Order of the Knights of St. John of Jerusalem in England. The Hospitaller house at Halston in Shropshire, which had been the administrative centre for all Hospitaller estates in North Wales, had changed hands several times by the time Mary came to throne. But the appointment of a preceptor of Halston when the order was revived in England in 1558 seems to have had no practical effect. Mary's reign lasted only five years and when her half-sister Elizabeth became Queen the country became Protestant once more and the Knights of the Hospital of St. John left England again, this time for good.

In 1522 Suliman had driven the Hospitallers from Rhodes and in 1565 he prepared to repeat his success in Malta. This time the Knights of Malta withstood the might of Suliman's army for four months until long delayed reinforcements arrived from Sicily and the Turks fled.

By the time of the French Revolution the Order of the Hospital was in decline. On his way to invade Egypt the Emperor Napoleon landed in Malta and easily took the island. On 11th June 1798 the Hospitallers surrendered and were given just three days to gather their personal possessions and leave. Six days later the French also left, but took with them everything of value they could find—and there was much. All the treasure accumulated by the Hospitallers over the 800 years of their existence was loaded onto Napoleon's flagship, *L'Orient*, but Napoleon was not to enjoy his spoils. On 1st August his ships were destroyed by Nelson's fleet at the Battle of the Nile and the Hospitallers' treasure was lost to the waters of Aboukir Bay.

Once again the Order was homeless and once more the brothers dispersed to find refuge where they could. In 1834 new headquarters were set up in Rome, and the Hospitallers abandoned the military side of the Order to concentrate upon the care of the sick and the poor, just as the first Brothers of the Order of the Hospital of St. John of Jerusalem had done more than 700 years before. In Britain the St. John Ambulance Association was founded in 1877 to provide ambulance transport and first aid instruction to the public. Then ten years later the St. John Ambulance Brigade was formed as an organisation of trained volunteers who provided first aid and ambulance transport at public events. The Brigade was recognised by Queen Victoria in 1888 as a Royal Order of Chivalry with the title The Venerable Order of the Hospital of St. John of Jerusalem, to which King George V added 'Most'. The primary aim of the Order that began in Jerusalem in the 11th century has continued for almost a thousand years. Today we know them as members of the St. John's Ambulance Brigade and immediately recognise them at public events, as they care for spectators and participants, by the eight-pointed white cross of the Hospitallers on their uniform.

The Poor Knights of the Temple of Solomon

Various sources differ over the number of crusaders who remained to guard the roads to Jerusalem and the date when they actually commenced their work. Many state nine, others 30. In either event it was small, but the sources agree that Hugh de Paynes was their leader. They took the accustomed monastic triple vow of poverty, chastity and obedience but in the case of the Templars the vow was of *obedience*, poverty and chastity because their first and most important duty was to *obey* the orders of their Grand Master, while the vow of poverty was made as an individual promise which did not apply to the Order as a whole. A Templar knight was never held for ransom, it would never have been paid.

Concerned by the lack of men under his command to control the newly taken land, King Baldwin II realised that if the Templars were recognised by the pope they would gain prestige and attract more knights to their service. In 1126 Baldwin wrote to Abbot Bernard of Clairvaux, asking for his help in promoting the Templars' cause with the pope. Bernard was known throughout Europe not only as a great spiritual leader, for his advice was sought and applied by kings and popes. The Abbot of Clairvaux was probably well aware of the work of the Templars, for his uncle André de Montbard was one of the knights who had remained in the Holy Land to guard the pilgrim routes, and land for the monastery at Clairvaux had been donated by one of their newest members, Count Hugh of Champagne. Not surprisingly André was chosen to deliver King Baldwin's letter to his nephew.

Bernard was greatly impressed with the idea of a monastic group devoted to fighting for Christ and he immediately agreed to lend his support and contacted the pope, who had been one of his pupils. Pope Honorius II personally agreed with the proposal and made arrangements for the matter to be debated. When the good news reached Jerusalem a small group of Templars led by Hugh de Paynes set off for Rome. There they received an audience with Pope Honorius and were able to furnish first-hand accounts of the protection they were providing in the Holy Land. They then left for France where the important debate concerning their future was to take place at the Council of Troyes.

It was January 1128 when the Council of Troyes convened. The pope's representative, Cardinal Matthew of Albano, presided over the assembly of archbishops, bishops, abbots, including Bernard of Clairvaux, and powerful local landowners. Cardinal Matthew invited Hugh de Paynes to address the council. After describing the events leading up to the taking of Jerusalem, he went on to tell of the group of knights who had remained in the Holy Land to protect pilgrims travelling the roads to Jerusalem. He concluded by explaining that in order for the work to continue they needed official recognition from the pope, a structure for their daily routine, and support in the way of men and money. The members of the council, being considerably impressed with Hugh's words, greatly influenced by Bernard's support, and probably already briefed by the pope of his own approval, agreed that the Templars should be granted their requests. Until this time the Templars had worn their own clothes with no uniformly recognisable items and now, along with his recognition of their Order, the pope specified that the knights should wear white habits while other members of the Order should wear brown or black.

The pope's approval was of the utmost importance for this new Order, which was unlike any other monastic order as its members were fighting men whose purpose was to kill other men. This was an immensely difficult concept, not only for the Christian Church to accept but for the knights themselves, as each time an enemy was killed they were breaking Christ's Commandment 'Thou shalt not kill'. The Rule that would eventually structure the life of the members of the new order would need to differ from that of the Benedictine, Augustine and Cistercian Orders. Fasting would not be sensible for men who could be called to battle at a moment's notice and time would have to be assigned for the practice of battle skills and for the care of horses and equipment. Great discretion would be necessary in setting out the Rule of the Temple, and Bernard of Clairvaux was the just the man to do this. When the Rule was completed it contained 72 clauses, but eventually grew to contain 686 clauses. The final paragraph was one of the most important as it stated that all the clauses were to be implemented 'at the discretion of the Master'. The Rule of the Temple was at its conception concerned solely with the Kingdom of Jerusalem, for as yet there were no other Templar houses. In due course, however, each country would have its own Master, with the Grand Master of the Temple at Jerusalem in overall control of the Order.

After the Council of Troyes, Hugh de Paynes did not return to Jerusalem immediately but set off through France and thence England and Scotland. By the close of the Council meeting at Troyes three properties in France had already been gifted to the new Order and Hugh was seeking not just more grants, but also men ready to follow him. According to the *Anglo-Saxon Chronicles* 'He summoned folk out to Jerusalem, and then with him went so many folk as never before nor since the first journey in Pope Urban's day'.

The Templars continued to receive gifts for the rest of their existence. The revenue they raised from the lands they farmed and the monetary donations received were essential to keep their brothers well equipped in the Holy Land. Crusading was an expensive business. Men and animals had to be well housed and regularly fed; tents and clothing, arms and armour did not last forever in good condition and would continually need to be repaired and regularly replenished; the care of horses, mules and camels did not come cheap and the animals had a limited life expectancy, they would frequently need to be replaced. These and the many other expenses involved to ensure successful campaigns created a constant need for funds which the Templar estates throughout Europe amply provided.

But one problem remained—every time they caused the death of a foe they committed a sin by breaking one of the Commandments, yet they were doing Christ's work as approved by the pope. In 1135 Bernard provided the solution by writing a long letter, *De Laude*, 'In Praise', to Hugh, in which he assured the Knights of the Temple that the men they put to death were the enemies of Christ and by killing them the Templars were ridding the world of evil. They were warrior monks, the knights of Christ. Once Bernard's ideas were circulated they were widely accepted and the Templars gained even more credibility. Hugh de Paynes died the following year having spent 40 years of his life in the Holy Land, 18 of them as founder and Master of the Temple in Jerusalem. It was under the leadership of his successor, Robert de Craon, that the Templars received *Omne Datum Optimum*, 'Every Best Gift', from Pope Innocent II. This effectively made them answerable only to the pope and therefore free from all other ecclesiastical demands. Originally chaplains from outside the Order had been appointed by local bishops to conduct all worship in Templar houses but now chaplain-brothers were added to the ranks of the

Templars, which set them free from diocesan control. Succeeding popes followed Innocent's example, reaffirming *Omne Datum Optimum* and usually adding gifts of their own; in time the Templars were even allowed to build their own churches and cemeteries.

The Rule of the Temple had banned any ornamentation of clothing or weapons but in 1147, on the eve of the Second Crusade, Pope Eugenius III gave the Templars a special gift—their very own logo. The knights already wore the white of purity and now they were given a cross in the red of martyrdom which was to be worn on the left breast of their white robes.

The Templar Rule lists five classes of Brothers of the Order. The aristocratic knights, who had been trained since boyhood in the ways of chivalry and warfare, and who were now privileged to wear the white mantle with its red cross, became the warriors and governors of the Order. Next in rank came the sergeants or serving brothers, men of free birth who, although not entitled to wear the white mantle, were light-armed troops who also acted as squires to the knights and attendants to the high officials of the Order. Minor officials fulfilled a variety of duties including managing the smaller houses and rural estates. The chaplains of the Order took care of the spiritual lives of the Templars and were probably the most highly educated of the brothers, and lastly there were manual workers who performed both skilled and menial services. Associates and temporary members, including married brothers, were those who joined the Order for a short time only, some when they were on Crusade or on pilgrimage in the Holy Land and some, who were on the point of death, for the salvation of their souls.

It was during the Second Crusade, 1147–1149, that the Templars first fought together in battle, as distinct from fighting bandits and highwaymen on the pilgrim routes. They were superbly trained, well-disciplined, efficient knights fighting as a united force, not as individuals, who rallied to their 'piebald' standard of black and white, black signifying the sin-ridden life they had left behind, white the purity of a life spent fighting for Christ. The leader of the Second Crusade, King Louis VII of France, immediately recognised the Templars' skill and discipline and placed his army under their control. Even so the Second Crusade ended in failure when the crusaders were not only unsuccessful in their siege of Damascus, but were forced into an humiliating retreat.

In July 1187 the Hospitallers and Templars were part of the crusader force destroyed at the the battle of the Horns of Hattin after being lured into a trap by the Muslim leader Saladin. Noblemen were ransomed and their soldiers sold into slavery, but the Hospitaller and Templar knights, who would never convert to Islam and could never be ransomed, were beheaded on the spot. Saladin then went on to take Jerusalem on 2 October, but unlike the crusaders in 1099 was gracious in victory—there were no revenge killings and no church was destroyed. But he did ensure that the Templar headquarters were thoroughly cleansed until all traces of Christian occupation had been eradicated and it was fit to become once more the al-Aqsa Mosque. With the loss of Jerusalem the Hospitallers and Templars set up their new headquarters at Acre.

In 1191 King Richard I of England and King Philip II of France became leaders of the Third Crusade after the original leader, Barbarossa, had fallen from his horse and drowned while crossing a river. In July Richard and Philip relieved the city of Acre and proudly flew their banners from the city walls. A few weeks later Philip left for France. Richard led the crusaders towards Jerusalem but in the end decided not to attack the city, instead negotiating a treaty with Saladin in which it was agreed that Christian pilgrims would be allowed to visit the Holy Sepulchre in Jerusalem, and securing a strip of coastal plain some 100 miles long, stretching from Jaffa to Acre. Acre had the best protected, deep water harbour and busiest port on the east Mediterranean coast, yet just a hundred years later it was lost, ending the Christian occupation of *Outremere*.

The loss of the Holy Land was a great blow not least to the Templars, but soon they had more personal problems to deal with. In 1307 the King of France accused the Knights of the most abominable behaviour. The attack appears to have been completely unexpected and unwarranted but its royal instigator had obviously carefully planned and then expertly carried out his attack on the Order.

King Philip IV of France was known as *le Bel*, the Fair, the sobriquet acquired from his handsome face, not from his disposition. He and Pope Boniface had had many disagreements but things came to a head in 1296 when Philip, who was always in need of funds, decided to tax all church properties in France. The pope was furious and issued his claim that 'All human beings (including kings and emperors) should be subject to the Pontiff of Rome'. Philip arranged to have the pope kidnapped and the deed was successfully carried out by his right-hand man Nogaret. Incensed at such an outrage the local people soon set Boniface free but a month later he was dead, supposedly from self-inflicted injuries. Pope Benedict, Boniface's successor, died after only nine months as pope, after having accidentally eaten some poisoned figs soon after a disagreement with King Philip. Philip then contrived to ensure that the next pope was a Frenchman and Pope Clement V was duly installed in the new papal residence at Avignon in the south of France.

In 1306 Philip had another idea for acquiring money. He sent out orders to his officials all over France instructing that every Jew in France should be arrested and sent into exile, and their property seized for the crown. It was a very successful fund-raising exercise and perhaps a rehearsal for Philip's next project when his target was the Order of the Temple of Solomon.

Early in 1307 the Grand Master of the Temple, Jacques de Molay, had arrived in style at the French port of Marseilles on his way to meet with the pope to discuss plans for the next crusade. The Grand Master of the Hospital had also been invited but he was fully occupied in Rhodes fighting for control of that island. Throughout the year Jacques de Molay attended meetings, some concerning the possible amalgamation of the Templar and Hospitaller Orders, and was present at many civil and court functions. The Grand Master was obviously completely unaware of King Philip's plans for his arrest and the ruin of the Templars.

In September 1307 King Philip's officials throughout France received sealed orders that were not to be opened until the evening of 12 October. On the morning of Friday 13 October 1307 every Templar in France was to be arrested, including the Grand Master of the Order. It should have been a different story this time—the Jews had had no defenders but the Templars were answerable only to the pope. Philip had no right to arrest them

Jacques de Molay,
from a 13th-century illustration

and they were entitled to legal protection. But such details did not bother the King of France, and he wasn't expecting any trouble from 'his' pope. The Templars were charged with a whole range of offences which included denying Christ, spitting on the Cross, sodomy and idolatry. All these charges would help to disgrace them and bring down their Order, but the main charge against them was heresy. Heresy was a popular accusation in the 12th and 13th centuries. In 1184 Pope Lucius III had created the earliest episcopal inquisition by ordering his bishops to make systematic enquiry, *L'inquisitio*, into any deviation from the official teaching of the church. Once the charge of heresy was made the chances of escaping death were almost nil and the ultimate penalty was to be burned at the stake. In 1252 Pope Innocent IV sanctioned torture as a means to discover heresy, a policy not abolished until 1816.

At the time of the Templars' trial the use of torture was at its height and the men involved in its application were expert at forcing confessions. Sinners who confessed and repented were given a penance and absolution, but for those who had admitted to a crime only to later retract their confession the only punishment was to be burnt at the stake.

Towards the end of November the pope suddenly became interested in the case against the Templars. He ordered all Christian rulers throughout Europe to arrest every Templar and to take possession of all Templar properties. King Edward I of England had died in July 1307 and his son became King Edward II. The new king had initially supported the Templars against the charges made by Philip, but on receipt of the pope's instructions 135 Templars were arrested and imprisoned, among whom were six knights and eleven priests. Edward managed to treat the Templars as leniently as possible and refused to use torture. The pope put pressure on Edward by sending men from France who were skilled in seeking out heresy through torture, but no English Templars were tortured and none confessed.

Once Pope Clement had become involved there was no quick end to the trials in France, and the accused Templars were kept in dreadful conditions and suffered horrific tortures over the next five years. In 1310 the pope announced that he would hear any evidence in defence of the Order and many of the imprisoned Templars, including those who had been tortured, volunteered to come forward. This was definitely not part of Philip's plan and in order to make these volunteers think again he had 54 of the Templars who had retracted their confessions burned alive in a field outside Paris. There were no more offers to defend the Order. Even so it was not until April 1312 that a

Papal bull was drawn up which officially disbanded the Order of the Poor Knights of the Temple of Solomon, without finding it guilty of any crime. Except for four high-ranking officials—Jacques de Molay, the Grand Master of the Order, Geoffrey de Charnay, the Preceptor of Normandy, Geoffrey de Gonneville, the Preceptor of Aquitaine and Hugh de Peraud, who had been a Templar treasurer—all the remaining imprisoned Templars were to be judged by their provincial councils.

The final act in the trial of the Templars took place when the Grand Master was forced to make a public confession of his crimes. On 18 March 1314, in chains and wearing their Templar robes, the four high ranking officials were presented to a huge crowd outside Notre Dame Cathedral. Jacques de Molay, who was now in his 70s, was charged to repeat his confession to the waiting people, but what he said was not what they expected to hear. He told them that his confession had been made up of lies in order to avoid torture, and that the Order of the Knights of the Temple of Solomon was innocent of all the charges against it. Geoffrey de Charnay followed his Grand Master's example, retracting his own confession and declaring the innocence of the Order. The French officials had been taken completely by surprise, but before any more damage could be done the chained men were hurried away. King Philip then moved quickly. Later that same day Jacques de Molay and Geoffrey de Charnay were chained to stakes set up on an island in the River Seine, and slowly burned to death. It is said that as he suffered Jacques de Molay cursed the pope and the king, ordering them to appear before God before the end of the year; Pope Clement V died in April 1314, and King Philip IV in November 1314.

The reason for King Philip's action against the Templars has never been satisfactorily explained.

Hospitallers & Templars in England & Wales

The *Anglo-Saxon Chronicles* of 1128 record that in Normandy, 'King Henry I of England received Hugh [de Paynes] with much honour and gave him treasure of gold and silver and sent him on to England where he was received by all good men; all gave him treasure, in Scotland also, and sent by him much property all in gold and silver'. A wonderful response was given to Hugh's call for support and by 1135 Templar houses had been set up at Shipley in Sussex, Temple in Cornwall and Warwick.

Both Orders established their English headquarters in London. The Templars built their first London temple on land they had been given in Holborn. About 50 years later this was followed by their 'New Temple' built on a site between Fleet Street and the River Thames. The Hospitallers set up their headquarters on land they they had been given near the 'well of the clerks' and their site at Clerkenwell is now home to the Museum and Library of the Order of St. John.

It is not easy to provide the dates of foundation, or the identities of the donors, of all the Templar and Hospitaller preceptories and commandaries in England and Wales. Even though a good deal of information is available, there are frequent discrepancies, omissions and differing opinions. The Templar property in Garway, Herefordshire, is an excellent example of the difficulties encountered pinning down dates and donors, or even the recipients of the gifts.

Sometime in the 12th century a gift of land in Garway was made to the Knights Templar, but so far no charter has come to light giving details of the date or the name of the donor. It is clear that the date of the gift must be later than 1128, when the Order was officially recognised by the pope, but earlier than a charter that gave the Templars permission to clear their land in Garway. Unfortunately this charter is not precisely dated, the only clue being the presence of Richard, Bishop of Winchester, who held the position from 1173 to 1189 and witnessed the document. This gives a range of 61 years maximum in which to identify the donor. The generosity of the gift—at least 2,000 acres—meant that the donor was rich and presumably powerful, a category that would include kings and leading Marcher lords.

If King Henry I had made the first gift of land in England to the Templars it surely would have been worthy of record, but as Lees in *Records of the Knights Templar in the 12th century* notes, 'in England nothing is certainly known of the history of the Templars between their arrival in 1128 and Queen Mathilda's grant of Cressing Temple [Essex] in 1137'. After Henry I's death the country was plunged into civil war as his daughter, the Empress Mathilda, fought with her cousin Stephen for the crown of England. According to the *Anglo-Saxon Chronicles* it was a time when Christ and His angels slept. King Stephen's father, Stephen de Blois, had died while on the First Crusade, and his wife, another Mathilda, was the niece of Godfrey de Bouillon and his brother Baldwin, the first two Christian rulers of Jerusalem. It is not surprising, therefore, that in the year after she became queen, Mathilda granted the manor of Cressing to the Knights Templar and two years later gave them Cowley in Oxfordshire. Other landowners quickly followed their queen's example and by the end of Stephen's reign Templar estates had been established in Balsall, Warwickshire; Bisham, Berkshire; Eagle and Willoughton, Lincolnshire; East Cowton, Penhill and Temple Hirst, Yorkshire; Lannock and Temple Dinsley, Hertfordshire; Temple Guiting, Gloucestershire; Trebeigh, Cornwall and Witham in Essex. The many grants made during Stephen's reign appear to have been well documented but there is no mention of Garway.

King Henry II also had connections with Jerusalem and the Crusaders. His paternal grandfather, Falk of Anjou, had been the fourth King of Jerusalem; his uncle was King Baldwin III of Jerusalem, and his wife, Eleanor of Aquitaine, had been on the Second Crusade with her first husband, King Louis VII of France. During Henry II's reign the Templars acquired more land from various landowners in Britain and set up their houses at Aslackby and South Witham in Lincolnshire; Denney, Cambridgeshire; Llanmadog, Glamorgan; Lydley Heys, Shropshire; Merton, Oxfordshire; Temple Bruer, Lincolnshire; Temple Combe, Somerset; Temple Ewell, Kent and Temple Newsam in West Yorkshire. According to Lees, 'Henry it seems was lavish of privileges, immunities and franchises though somewhat sparing of land grants to the Templars and apparently founded no preceptory in England. He gave rights of assart in Royal Forests and the advowsons of churches in royal

Interior of the13th-century 'barley' barn at Cressing Temple, Essex

patronage and confirmed many charters of former donors, but he alienated comparatively little of Crown land and strengthened the Order as an administrative organisation of a highly privileged kind rather than a territorial power'.

In a charter witnessed by Richard Bishop of Winchester, Henry II formally recognised the rights of various Templar properties to forests they had cleared:

> *Henricus Dei gratia Rex Anglie etc. salutem. Sciatis me concessisse et hac presenti Carta nostra confirmasse fratribus milicie templi Jerusalem quietanciam de essartis de subscriptis terris, videlicet de m.m. acris terre in Walliis apud Garewi ...'.* [Henry, by the Grace of God, King of England etc. greetings. Know that I have granted and by this our present charter confirmed to the brethren of the Knights of the Temple of Jerusalem quittance of assarts of the following lands, that is 2,000 acres of land in Wales at Garway ...]

followed by a list of other Templar properties.

This document has often been used to date the gift of land to the Templars, but it reads as permission to assart, that is to clear the land. This was an important gift in its own right as hunting is known to have been important to the Norman kings. Hunting had always been popular but the Conqueror brought it into a new dimension—any land deemed to be forest (and thus in royal hands) also included everything in it. He drew up forest laws that were applied in order to protect the venison and vert, the latter being the trees and bushes that made up the necessary habitat. Absolutely nothing was allowed to interfere with royal enjoyment of the hunt.

The earliest architectural evidence of the Templar church at Garway dates to the 12th century, but not precisely enough to know if the land on which it is built was given during Henry's reign (1154–1189), or earlier. King Richard confirmed his father's charter, between 6th July and 31st December 1189 and infers that the grant was Henry's:

> Richard, by the grace of God, King of England etc., greetings. Know that we have granted and by this our present charter confirmed in perpetual alms to God and Saint Mary and the brethren of the Knights of the Temple of Solomon for our salvation, and Eleanor our mother, and for the soul of King Henry our father ... for the following gifts which our father gave them, that is ... all the land of Garway with the castellario which was Herman's and with all its appurtenances.

Who else might have made the original grant? One of the most powerful Marcher families was that of Walter de Lacy and like many other landowners he made gifts of land to the church. He was actually inspecting work on St. Peter's church in Hereford when he fell to his death in 1085. Walter was succeeded first by his son Roger, who was disgraced by rebelling against the king, and then by his son Hugh, whose daughter Sibilla married Payn fitz John, an important official at the court of King Henry I.

Payn was the king's chamberlain; he was witness to many documents of the time and held important posts in Hereford and Shropshire. Such services were rewarded by gifts of land and Payn became a wealthy man. He became even richer when, after Hugh de Lacy's death in 1115, the king allowed the Lacy lands to pass to Payn through his wife Sibilla. At some time Payn exchanged the castles of Grosmont, Whitecastle and Skenfrith with Henry I, for land in Archenfield. This was before 1137 as that was the year in which they both died. Soon after his death Payn's daughter Cecilie married Roger the son of Miles of Gloucester. In a document dated December 1137 King Stephen makes a 'Confirmation of all the lands of his wife's father, Pagan fitz John' to Roger. Among the properties listed as having been in Payn's possession are Archenfield and Garway, which means that he, or Roger and Cecilie, could be considered as possible Templar benefactors. However, until proof positive turns up there is nothing to identity conclusively the person who made the gift of 2,000 acres of land in Garway to the Knights of the Temple of Solomon.

The brothers of the Orders were virtual Lords of the Manor. Doris Stenton, in *English Society in the Early Middle Ages*, explains that the word manor came to mean 'an estate which was an economic unit, in which all the tenants were bound to the lord and his demesne farm, his free tenants paying him rent for their land and helping him at busy seasons; his unfree tenants doing weekly labour service; and all of them regularly attending his court of justice, his hall moot, for the settlement of their quarrels and for the regulation of communal affairs'. Like all lords of the manor, the Templars and Hospitallers employed senechals or stewards to hold the courts and deal with all matters arising there and bailiffs to collect the rents.

The size of land grants to the Templars and Hospitallers in England and Wales varied enormously, from huge estates to smaller manors and even smaller *camerae* (see below). Some of the largest grants to the Templars were lands in Yorkshire and Lincolnshire where they made huge profits from their flocks of sheep. Stenton writes, 'the twelfth-century sheep were hardworking animals, prized for their dung for tillage, the ewes' milk for cheese, their skin for parchment, and above all for their wool'. A.L. Poole confirms, in *From Domesday Book to Magna Carta* that 'the sheep were the animals of the greatest utility, and a hundred, it was calculated, would add £1 a year to the profits of the farm'. In the records of 1308–1338, the Templar estate in Willoughton, Lincolnshire, which was the richest of the Knights Templar houses in England, raised £284. In the records of 1535 the estate at Melchbourne, Bedfordshire was the richest of the Hospitaller properties and raised £241.

The profits made by the smaller properties were obviously less and ranged between £40 and £10. The smallest properties of the Orders were *camerae*, a name given to small estates connected with the Knights Hospitaller. Literally the word means 'vaulted room', from the Greek *kamara*, and may derive from the room in which accounts were recorded before being despatched to Clerkenwell.[3] These small estates, 'were probably run by a salaried bailiff who occupied the 'camera' or hall, organized the work of a small demesne labour force, and collected rents from the tenant farmers'.[4]

Whilst the properties were being run by both Orders to give the utmost support to their brothers in the Holy Land, like all medieval religious houses they had other functions. Travellers, not only those on pilgrimage, relied upon abbeys, preceptories and commandaries as safe places to spend a night or longer. They were assured of a generous welcome and knew that food and a place to sleep would be freely provided as well as stabling for their horses, but a stay of three days was generally regarded as the maximum to be expected. Also among the brothers in the Templar and Hospitaller houses would be found *corrodaries*, 'pensioners', permanent residents who, having made substantial gifts to the Order, could spend the rest of their lives there and would be buried in the cemetery, assured of the prayers of the brothers.

The medieval world was full of tithes and tolls but the Templars and Hospitallers were given several dispensations by popes and kings, which freed them from many of these every-day taxes. In 1137 the Hospitallers were given exemption from the payment of tithes 'because all your goods should be devoted to the support of the poor and pilgrims and should not therefore be applied to other uses'. The Templars were released from the payment of tithes two years later, 'Since those who defend the church should live and be supported by the goods of the church, we entirely prohibit the extraction of tithes against your will from your moveable or moving property or from anything belonging to your venerable house'.

Freedom from tithes continued to be granted to both Templars and Hospitallers by successive popes and kings and this benefit was also enjoyed by their tenants who, in order to identify their privilege, marked their homes with crosses. This desirable state led to abuse of the system and developed to such an extent that King Edward I was forced to take action. He prohibited the unauthorised use of the cross by people who were not Templar or Hospitaller tenants and the guilty forfeited their land.

The pope also gave the Templars permission to build their own churches and to bury the dead in their own churchyards, burial fees providing additional income. Henry II exempted both Orders from *amercement*, fines and punishment in royal courts, and his son, King Richard I, freed them from many tolls such as *pontage*—bridge tolls, and *pavage*—a tax for the upkeep of paved roadways. In 1246 the pope ordained that neither Templars nor Hospitallers could be prevented by a bishop from converting church tithes to their own use. Henry III, in a charter of 1253, granted the Templars many privileges including *sac*—the right to hold a court, and *tol*—the right of jurisdiction of offenders within the manor. Many of the forest regulations were not applied to them, and they were also free of port dues, and did not pay tolls on goods in the king's market and fairs.

With so many estates in the west the Templars, through necessity, became experts at moving money and goods to the east. They acquired their own fleet and extended their enterprise by carrying pilgrims on journeys out to, and back from, Jerusalem thus continuing to fulfil their original purpose. The Templar expertise was quickly recognised and utilised by wealthy and powerful men who needed to transfer their money and valuables safely to other countries. The Knights of the Temple soon became international bankers but, unlike the Jewish bankers who were often condemned for usury because of the high interest they extorted, charged only for the service they provided, taking into account the time taken and the risks involved.

Not only respected for their business acumen, the Templars were trusted as envoys and advisors by popes and kings, and many examples of this trust can be found. For instance, when Henry II of England and Louis VII of France were at loggerheads over the possession of two castles in the Vexin, the Templars were given the right to hold these castles until an agreement was reached. When King Stephen signed the settlement agreeing that Mathilda's son Henry should be his successor, a Templar was among the list of witnesses. In 1164, Richard de Hastings, Master of the Temple in England, was involved, with the Bishops of Salisbury and Norwich and the Earls of Leicester and

Cornwall, in an attempt to reconcile Henry II and Thomas Beckett. Another Master of the Temple in England, Aymeric de St. Maur, was a faithful advisor to King John especially in the contest with the barons which led up to the signing of the Magna Carta. Both King John and his son Henry III relied heavily upon the Templars for a variety of service and advice and were frequent guests at the London Temple and other Templar houses. In 1260 Simon de Montfort and the leading barons met in the Temple to discuss the action to be taken against King Henry III. The Templars were fighting with Edward I in the Scottish campaign, 1298–1299, when the Master of the Temple in England, Brian de Jay, was killed at the battle of Falkirk.

The London Temple was often used as a convenient venue for political and ecclesiastical meetings. In 1299 Edward I summoned Parliament to meet there, and between 1256 and 1299 the English clergy met there at least nine times to discuss various problems. Prominent men, papal legates, bishops and foreign diplomats found the Temple a convenient, and presumably a very comfortable lodging place when in London. Not only people were housed there; the Temple served as a royal and papal treasury where valuables and money could be safely held until they were needed. King John placed the Crown Jewels at the Temple for safe-keeping soon after becoming king and his son Henry III took the same precautions during the Barons' Revolt in 1261. Bishop Langton, treasurer to King Edward I, deposited £50,000 in silver plus gold and jewels in the Temple Treasury, which was later given to Piers Gaveston by Edward II. During his reign Henry II made grants of up to three casks of wine and five to ten deer from the Royal Forests to the Templars' Annual Chapter Meeting at the London Temple. Similar grants were conferred by Henry's successors, King John, King Henry III and King Edward I, who repeatedly authorised the Templars to take timber from the Royal Forests for use in the construction of new buildings and the repair of existing ones.

When Pope Clement V abolished the Order of the Knights of the Temple in 1312, most of their property was transferred to the Order of the Knights of the Hospital, but it was not that simple. Rulers of the countries involved were in no hurry to hand over the Templar lands now in their charge, and there were the expenses of the prisoners plus the cost of trials and executions to be calculated and deducted from the estates. In England in 1324 an Act of Parliament was passed ordering that the Templar lands be passed to the Hospitallers and in 1338 the Grand Master of the Hospitallers, Elyan de Villanova, directed Prior Philip de Thame to produce a report of the Hospitaller properties in England.

Hospitallers and Templars in Herefordshire

The Brothers of the Temple and the Hospital ran their estates in Europe with the sole purpose of financing their Orders' work in the Holy Land, and subsequently elsewhere.

Not all the gifts to the Orders were of large estates, some were smaller parcels of land, others were individual dwellings in villages, towns or cities. Many were rented out at statutory rates but very little information is given about such properties in the financial accounts other than the amounts collected by the bailiffs, which are often grouped together under *Reditus Assisus*, the income from rent to a landlord. Arable land was valued per acre according to its quality, and the price for pasture was usually calculated according to the number and type of animals grazing there. 'As a general rule sheep paid one penny per head, an ox rather more than a horse, the calf at about half, the cow twice as much as the ox'.[5] Although they were monks, the Hospitallers and Templars did not build monasteries on their newly acquired land in England and Wales. A typical estate managed by brothers of the Orders would be similar to that of any medieval country manor, consisting of a house surrounded by farmland with additional buildings such as a church, a dovecot, barns, stables and workshops. Brothers of the Hospital and Temple may have begun their lives in such places, but their life in the Holy Land had not provided them with the experience that was necessary on their return. However they soon adapted to the new way of life becoming proficient in animal husbandry, experts at accountancy and superb organisers in the transportation of money, new recruits, horses and supplies to their brothers in *Outremere*.

There was one property in Herefordshire which would have conformed to the monastic plan—the convent at Aconbury, which had connections with the Hospitallers. It was built by Margaret de Lacy who was the daughter of one powerful Marcher Lord, William de Braose, and wife of another, Walter de Lacy. De Braose had been loyal to King Richard and became a favourite of King John, who arranged the marriage between Margaret and Walter in November 1200. Margaret's father gained the epithet 'the Ogre of Abergavenny' for a particularly brutal act, even for those days. In 1175 he invited Seisyll and other local Welsh leaders to a Christmas banquet at his castle in Abergavenny. When the Welshmen arrived at the castle they were welcomed by de Braose, a genial and unarmed host. Encouraged to enjoy the festivities similarly unarmed, they agreed to leave their weapons outside the hall, but William de Braose's outward show of friendliness masked his seething hatred. Once his guests were relaxed and off guard he gave a signal to his own men who swiftly and efficiently murdered the Welshmen. Even this was not enough for the Marcher Lord who then sent his men to kill Seisyll's wife and seven-year-old son. Years later the king and de Braose fell out. De Braose managed to escape to France, but his wife and son, another William, were starved to death in Windsor Castle.

Margaret de Lacy prevailed upon King John to give her land on which she could build a house of nuns in memory of her father, mother and brother. Just before his death in 1216, the king relented and gave her 'three carucates of land to be assarted and cultivated in our forest of Aconbury for the establishment of a house of nuns who are to pray for the repose of her father, William de Braose, her mother Maud and her brother William'. Margaret made the decision that the house at Aconbury should be attached to the Hospitaller preceptory at Dinmore, and the first women there were received into the Order and given the appropriate clothing. But Margaret hadn't appreciated that members of the Order of St. John were liable for service abroad, which didn't suit her purpose at all. She wrote to the pope asking that the nuns should be allowed to become members of the Augustinian Order, but the Hospitallers were against the proposal. Five years passed before the pope gave instructions that the sisters of the monastery of Aconbury should be freed from the Order of the Hospital of St. John of Jerusalem. Nothing more was heard of the controversy and the convent at Aconbury became a community of Augustinian nuns.

Hospitaller Property in Herefordshire

The five gifts made to the Hospitallers in Herefordshire were at Callow, Dinmore, Hereford, Sutton St. Michael and Wormbridge. Brothers of the Order lived and worked in the Commandery at Dinmore, but other properties were all rented out. Bailiffs were employed at three, Callow, Sutton and Wormbridge, to collect the rents for which they were each paid 30s a year.

In records for 1338 a church is mentioned at Callow, but there are no expenses shown and any income from it is included with the other rents from a dwelling and 2 carucates of run-down land, which altogether came to £6. The present Church of St. Mary at Callow was built in 1830 but the font is believed to have come from the original church.

At Sutton there were 350 acres of arable land, some pasture and an 'appropriated' church, 'whereby the religious house in effect took over the rectory and paid a priest to act as vicar (meaning substitute) to look after the parish and the cure of the souls' keeping all the endowments in favour of the church for themselves.[6] By paying the priest they were also entitled to the larger tithes. This was a usual practice, though needed the bishop's permission, and the clergy were well looked after. It was obviously worthwhile, as the 1338 accounts of Dinmore show an annual payment of £1 made to the Rector of Sutton St. Michael and an income of £10 received. For some reason the Hospitallers also received the small tithes at Sutton which were recorded as being worth £1 13s. 1d.

Hospitaller property in Wormbridge included 200 acres of arable land and some pasture. Rents were collected but there are no details of the house or houses. However that there was a house owned by the Hospitallers in Wormbridge is known from an important court case concerning the privilege of sanctuary. Since Christianity had arrived in Britain in the 6th century criminals had been allowed to claim sanctuary in a church, a privilege which continued, even with conditions made by various kings, until the 18th century. The right of sanctuary was limited to forty days during which they could not be forcibly removed. After this time they could decide whether to face trial or to leave the country forever, in which case they would be given safe conduct to the nearest port. All the church required was that fugitives should enter sanctuary without weapons and confess to their crimes, whilst all stolen goods were to be restored and debts to be repaid as soon as possible. While under God's protection in the church they were expected to behave well and submit to any penance made on them by the priest of the church.

In 1485, after stealing a brass pot and other household goods to the value of £3, a horse worth 6s. 8d. and some cash from Isabel Cutta's house, William Bongam, a labourer from Garway took refuge in a house at Wormbridge. The Sheriff of Hereford, Roger of Bodenham, forcibly took him from the house and threw him into prison. Bongam pleaded guilty but stated that the house in which he had taken refuge belonged to the Knights Hospitaller and demanded to be returned there. John Stoke, on behalf of the Hospitallers said that the house was, 'a parcel of the preceptory of Dinmore and that from time immemorial the Hospitallers have always had and still possess this privilege and liberty, to wit, that any man or woman coming to any house belonging to them to take refuge after felony committed, and demanding this privilege, shall have safety and protection for their life without disturbance from any officer of the King of England or of any other person'. The jury found that the house belonged to the Hospitallers who did have the privilege they claimed and presumably Bongam was returned to that house to decide whether to stand trial or to leave the country.

In Hereford the Hospitallers owned land just outside Widemarsh Gate, the north gate of the city, but there is a degree of confusion as to whether this is the piece of land on which Coningsby Hospital was subsequently developed. It is often stated that they had a hospital there but if they did it was not worthy of an entry in the 1338 Report, Philip de Thame, Prior of England, simply recording the property as consisting of 30 acres of land and 6 acres of meadow adjoining giving an income of £5. It is strange that a working hospital did not provide any details of income, and usually buildings owned and occupied by the Order had their value recorded. Even more difficult to understand is the fact that no expenses are claimed for clothing and feeding the brothers who would be needed to maintain the hospital, or the patients who were being cared for. In 1343 when the Black Friars wished to extend their buildings, they exchanged six acres of their land in Wellington near Dinmore for one acre of

The western side of Coningsby Hospital facing Widemarsh Street, from an old postcard

the Hospitallers' land in Hereford. Perhaps the land exchanged with the Blackfriars was simply referred to as land belonging to the 'Hospital', rather than using the full title of the Knights of the Hospital of St. John of Jerusalem, and misinterpreted as a hospital in later references. Such an example is shown in an entry in the Bishop's *Register* on 14th March 1347 of a writ to Bishop Trilleck to make a return of benefices appropriated to the Knights of St. John and of their other revenue in the Hereford diocese. The bishop affirmed in return that the Knights had a certain chapel 'commonly called a hospital', which from its poverty could not be taxed.

In the 17th century Mary Louisa Bevan wrote a pamphlet, which cost 6 groats, entitled *A Brief Sketch of ye Coningsbie Hospital. Coningsby Hospital also known as y ReddeCote Hospital 1614*. In its she writes: 'Now it soe chanced that among y Princelie Possessions of Sir Thomas [Coningsby] was an aunciente Monasterie in y Suburbs of Hereford formerlie appertaining to y Order of Blacke Friars. Here Sir Thomas occasionallie took up his Lodging and it was Doubtlese During one of his Sojournes here that he Formed ye Project which ultimatelie resulted in ye Edification of ye Coningsby Hospitall.' She doesn't refer to a previous hospital on the site having given Sir Thomas his inspiration.

The interior courtyard of Coningsby Hospital, looking north-west

Yet, the Royal Commission on Historical Monuments, in its inventory of 1932, records that parts of the hall and chapel of Coningsby Hospital date to the 13th century when the building 'was formally occupied by the Knights of St. John'. The west end of the hall, for example, has a 14th-century window of two trefoiled ogee lights with tracery, whilst the chapel retains a 13th-century coffin-lid with a plain incised cross. The buildings of the hospital are arranged around a quadrangle and are built of local red sandstone and stone roofing slates. In 1984 repairs were carried out mainly to the stonework to the front of the building and the bellcot, but unfortunately without any archaeological recording.

Whatever confusion there may be over Hospitaller connections with Coningsby Hospital, there is considerable certainty as regards their activity at Dinmore. This was the largest of the five Hospitaller properties in Herefordshire and was the administrative centre of the Order for an area covering Herefordshire and Shropshire. In 1188 the Archbishop of Canterbury, accompanied by Gerald of Wales, was on a tour of Wales in a quest for men to take up

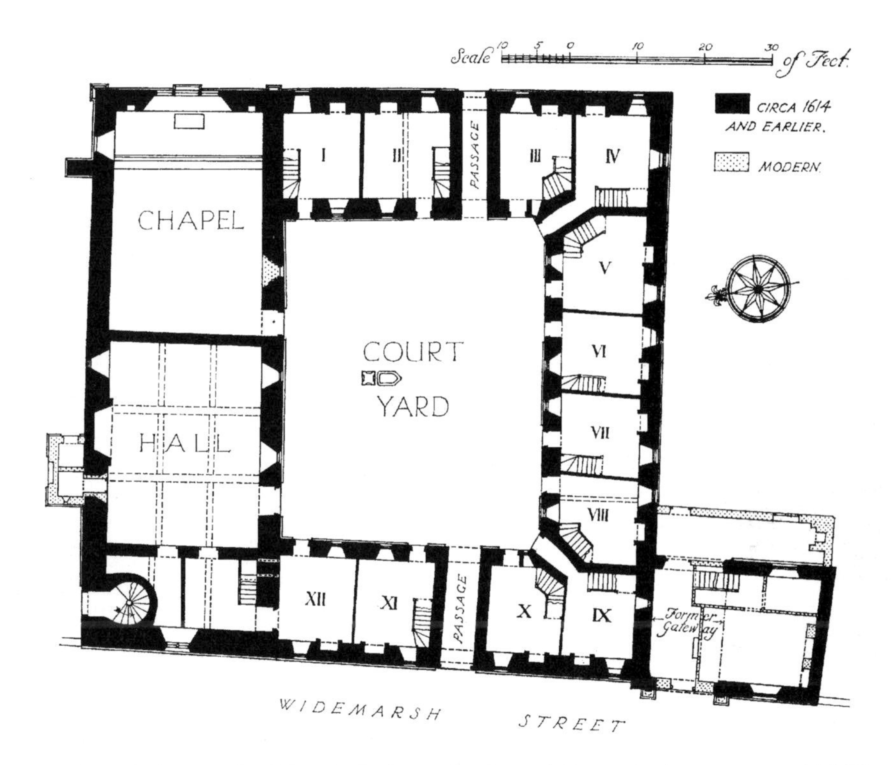

A plan of Coningsby Hospital, from the Royal Commission report of 1932

the cross for the Third Crusade. During their time at Hereford the Archbishop witnessed a grant of land in Dinmore to the Knights of the Hospital. The land belonged to a group of monks and it is thought that they, with William their Prior and Brother Thomas their founder, joined the Hospitallers as a result of hearing the Archbishop's appeal. Perhaps it is 'no coincidence that so many Hospitaller houses lie close to the great preaching tour'.[7]

The original grant at Dinmore was of about 100 acres, the land being surrounded by Royal Forests. In 1190 King Richard confirmed the grant: 'Let it be known that the Hospitaller Brothers of Jerusalem and all matters and possessions of theirs are under our care and protection. Also we have received into our care and protection Brother Thomas of Dinmore, and his brothers and all things and lands and possessions of his and of his place of Dunemora which with his assent we grant to the aforesaid Brothers of the Hospital, with one carucate of land as if it had been measured by legal knights of the county, in the time of our father, of our wood of Mawerthin as from the assarted road'.

In 1251 Henry III made a further grant to the Hospitallers giving them the right to hunt on their lands at Dinmore, quite a generous gesture knowing how important the forests were to the kings of England.

The Commandery at Dinmore became the most important Hospitaller house in the Marches and it was here that the Prior of London came on his annual visit to collect the funds raised from Hospitaller property in the area. Medieval work from the time of the Hospitallers remains in the basement of the house, and in part of the chapel. The Chapel of St. John of Jerusalem is built of local sandstone rubble and ashlar, the greater part of its north wall with its blocked round-headed doorway being dated to the foundation of the preceptory in 1189–90. About the middle of the 14th century the chapel was extended towards the east, possibly widened to the south and the west tower was inserted. The chancel retains a 14th-century east window, whilst two 13th-century coffin-lids have been reused in the fabric, one as a lintel of the squint in the north wall, the other as a lintel of the doorway to the tower's staircase, both retaining the remains of cross-heads carved into their surface. The earlier building formerly extended further to the west and may have had a nave. The chapel was restored in 1886. The dovecote, which was mentioned in 1338, was demolished about 1800 and the fishponds in the valley to the south of the chapel are now dry.

Some time after the Dissolution of the Monasteries King Edward VI granted lands to Sir Thomas Palmer which included Dinmore, and what became the manor house was substantially rebuilt. Sir Thomas had received much royal favour but even so he ended his life on the scaffold. The Patent Roll of Philip and Mary 1557 records that Queen Mary granted to Jane Russell, 'one of the gentlewomen of our Private Chamber all that enclosed site and precinct, late of the Preceptory of Dinmore in our county of Herefordshire with all rights, members and appurtenances lately being

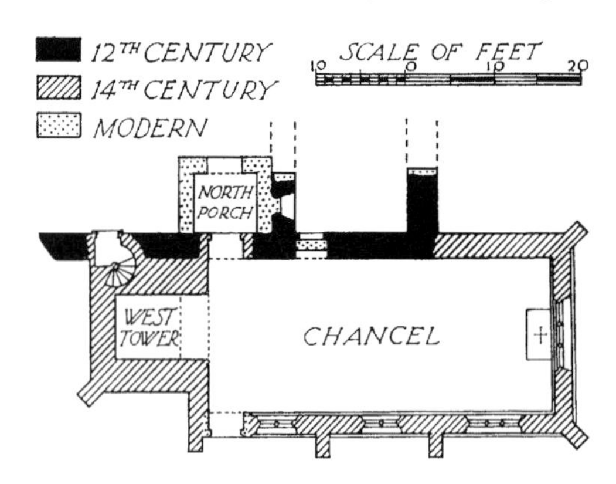

A plan of Dinmore chapel, from the Royal Commission report of 1932. The two buttresses on the north were originally parts of the walls of a range of buildings that extended to the north

parcel of the lands and possessions of Thomas Palmer, knight, attained and convicted of high treason; and also each and every house, building, dovecote, stable, structure, pond, fishpond, land and soil of ours within the said site or precinct of seven ambits in circumference being lately of the said Preceptory of Dynmore'. The gift was made to Jane Russell for life, and after her death would pass to her elder son Edward Russell until his death, when it would revert to the crown. The Wolrych family held the estate from the 16th century until it passed to the Flemings of Sibdon Castle, Shropshire. In 1788 Dinmore passed through marriage to the St. John family who lived there until 1927 when it was sold to Richard Hollins Murray.

It is possible to gain a valuable picture of the running of the Hospitaller estate at Dinmore from the 1338 Report by Prior Philip de Thame. Items for each property were given in the form of a balance sheet, which were usually set out in the same order for each property. The accounts also reveal the importance of *fraria*, a voluntary collection from the neighbourhood. £53 7s. 7d. was recorded under Dinmore, which was almost half the total income, all for the small expense of £1 6s. 8d. paid to the two clerks responsible for its collection; the total for the whole of England in 1338 was £888 4s. 3d.

The freedom from tithes and tolls that the Hospitallers and Templars enjoyed was an anathema to the Church and the collection of *fraria* must also have touched some nerves. Towards the end of the 13th century, when it was obvious that the Christians were losing the Holy Land to the Muslims, support for the Knights deteriorated and this is clearly shown in the Bishops' Registers of Hereford. In 1289 Bishop Swinfield received a Bull from Pope Nicholas who had been informed, upon reputable testimony, that after the lamentable capture of Tripoli certain Templars, Hospitallers and other Orders had been collecting alms in the name of their Orders for the fight in the Holy Land but were converting the funds to their own use. The pope therefore forbade the collection of such alms to all save those who should, after this prohibition, have special licences for the purpose committed to them by the Apostolic See.

In January 1291 the Archbishop of Canterbury sent out a letter to his bishops concerning a Papal Bull, in which he pointed out that although the pope appeared to have banned the collection of all alms, 'this in no wise covered the accustomed offerings called *fraria*, which had been regularly collected for the Order of St. John by its accredited agents'. The Archbishop went on to decree that the Hospitallers be allowed to continue to make collection of these voluntary offerings. The Bishop of Hereford followed the instruction of his Archbishop and allowed the collection of *fraria* in his diocese.

In October 1346 the collection of *fraria* was once again threatened and Bishop John de Trilleck received both an official and a private letter from the Archbishop of Canterbury. In the first the clergy and officials throughout the province were asked to commend to their people the Prior and Order of St. John of Jerusalem, and to permit the Order's agents to collect alms. National sentiment was then running against the Order, for the French Master and his knights had fought with the King of France against the English at the recent Battle of Crecy. The Archbishop pointed out that this was not to be held against the whole Order but had been a personal decision taken by the French Prior. Bishop Trilleck passed on the directions of the Archbishop and recommended the Order to the benevolence of his diocese. (When the Orders were first established, their whole reason for taking up arms was to fight for Christ in defence of the Christian Faith. But, as has been mentioned, during the following years both Orders had taken part in battles that were nothing to do with the Church, supporting both King Stephen and the Empress Mathilda during the Anarchy, both sides during the Barons' Revolt against the monarchy, and had fought against the Scots with King Edward I and his son.)

In the list of annual income and expenditure for Dinmore that follows, a carucate, or hide, was originally the amount of land that could be ploughed in one year using one plough to support a family. It varied with the soil quality but was generally between 60 and 180 acres. A bovate was also a variable measure related to the amount of land an ox could plough in a year, generally reckoned to be between 7 to 32 acres.

Dinmore's Annual Income for the year 1338

A well built manor house with a garden valued at	13s. 4d.
A columbarium valued at	6s. 8d.
300 acres of land @ 8d.; 100 acres @ 6d.; 100 acres @ 4d. (rented out)	£14 3s. 4d.
Assessed rents (17 marks $^{1}/_{2}$d.)	£11 6s. 8$^{1}/_{2}$d.
Rents from various towns in Herefordshire, Gwent, Shropshire (26 marks 8s. 3d.)	£17 14s. 11d.
Demesne land at Multon (rented out)	£ 1 2s. 0d.
2 carucates of land rented out at Rorynton	£ 3 6s. 8d.
Church at Clya, with 1 carucate of land rented out	£ 1 13s. 4d.
Church at Callow, and 2 rundown carucates of land rented out	£ 3 0s. 0d.
Church at Oxenhall, with 4 bovates rented out	£10 0s. 0d.
30 acres of land and an adjoining meadow at Hereford	£ 5 0s. 0d.
Fulling mill at Dinmore	£ 2 10s. 0d.
Water mill at Dinmore	£ 1 16s. 8d.
Churches at Porkirie and Penmark (Glamorgan?)	£ 1 0s. 0d.
From the *fraria* (80 marks 11d.)	£53 7s. 7d.

Dinmore's Annual Expenses for the year 1338

For baking bread - 80qr. of corn @ 3s. and 10qr. of rye @ 2s.	£13 0s. 0d.
For brewing ale – 20qr. malted corn and 120qr. oats	£12 3s. 4d.
Flesh and fish with other necessities @ 6s. 8d. a week	£17 6s. 8d.
Robes, mantles and other necessities for the Preceptor and two brothers	£ 5 4s. 0d.
Corrodaries	
Gilbert Pauely	£ 1 8s. 0d.
Laurence of York	£ 2 0s. 0d.
Henry Clerk	18s. 0d.
John le Hert	13s. 4d.
William le Port	10s. 0d.
For the seneschal of Dinmore for holding courts and defending pleas	£ 1 6s. 8d.
For the seneschal of Multon and other parts of the Marches	£ 1 6s. 8d.
For 1 clerk recording & accounting at the courts throughout the whole bailiwick	6s. 6d.
For 1 clerk collecting rents at Ludlow and elsewhere outside the manor	13s. 4d.
For 2 clerks collecting the fraria (1 mark each)	£ 1 6s. 8d.
A robe for the Preceptor's squire	13s. 4d.
Wages & clothing for the storekeeper, chamberlain, cook, fisherman, & bailiff 10s. each	£ 2 10s. 0d.
Wages to two boys in attendance on the Preceptor 1/2 mark each	13s. 4d.
Wages for 2 pages and 1 washerwoman 3s. 3d. each	9s. 9d.
For 1 chaplain	£ 1 0s. 0d.
Wages for the tiler 10s., the reaper 6s. 8d.,the swineherd 5s., the gardener 5s., and the swineherd's boy 3s.	£ 1 9s. 8d.
For 1 chaplain at Sutton 20s., 1 bailiff at Sutton 30s., the bailiff at Rowlston 30s., and the bailiff at Wormbridge 30s.	£ 5 10s. 0d.
For wine, oil, wax candles and other necessities for the chapel (Dinmore?)	6s. 8d.
Payments to various persons	£ 2 18s. 8d.
Expenses of the Archdeacon's visit and ecclesiastical dues	£ 1 0s. 0d.
Expenses of the Prior's 4-day visit	£ 4 0s. 0d.
For the repair of houses throughout the bailiwick	£ 3 6s. 8d.

From what seems to be merely a list of expenses in the Report of 1338, a wealth of information can be gleaned. From the first three items it is easy to see that the provision of food and drink was the greatest expense for the house. 80qr. of corn equated to 1 ton of flour, which would have made 1,760 2lb. loaves. The Dinmore bakers were making around 67 loaves of bread a fortnight. At the same time the Dinmore brewer could have been making six or seven barrels of ale a week, each barrel containing 36 gallons, giving an amazing 216 to 252 gallons, which would have varied in strength from very strong ale to weak small beer.[8]

Details of the clothing that was supplied clearly shows that the estate was run by the Preceptor and two brothers of the Order, and that their domestic staff included a porter, a cook, a baker, a storekeeper, a chamberlain, the Dinmore steward, the Preceptor's esquire, two pages and a washerwoman. Also eating at *mensa fratrum*, the brothers' table, were four corrodaries, and the chaplain. The clerks mentioned may have lived in or, like the manual workers listed—the tiler, the hayward, the gardener, the swineherd and his boy—could have been tenants on the estate. Altogether, without including visitors, at least 21 people were being fed every day. Others have established that in aristocratic houses of the period, as much as a gallon of ale per a head per day was drunk, and that 'a cereal based diet of bread and pottage characterised peasant diet, with ale as the main drink'.[9] The amount of bread baked and ale brewed at Dinmore suddenly doesn't seem excessive!

All medieval manors included demesne land, which was utilised to provide food for the lord of the manor and his family. In the 1185 Templar Inquest demesne lands were largely ignored, and this may also apply to the 1338 list of Hospitaller estates, possibly confirmed by the lack of entries under Dinmore indicating the number of animals and the amount of fruit or vegetables used in the kitchen. It is interesting that some meat and fish was bought in even though a swineherd and his boy, and a fisherman were employed by the Order. Maybe an excessive number of travellers made the purchase of additional food necessary.

Rees' description of the Prior of Clerkenwell's annual visit to Slebach surely applied to the other main houses of the Order in each area including Dinmore. 'Accompanied by officers and grooms, his secretary and public notary, a full scale check was carried out on everything, relics, jewels, ornaments, books etc. They checked that Church Services were performed with decency and that the sacraments were administered properly. The name and value of every estate was recorded and the repairs needed were detailed. The visit was costly and came out of the local budget', which in Dinmore's case was £4. The annual visit by the Master of the Temple in London to Templar preceptories and commanderies in England was not dissimilar, although he would collect not only the money that had been raised but also any new members who had been recruited. He would be accompanied by his ministerial staff, his chancery of clerks, his chaplains and his attendant knights and squires.

Templar Property in Herefordshire

The Templars, like the Hospitallers, also received five gifts in Herefordshire. Their Preceptory at Garway was the administrative house of the Order for the area and they established another preceptory at Upleadon. Three smaller properties—St. Wulstan in Welsh Newton, Rowlestone and Harewood—were farmed out.

At St. Wulstan in Welsh Newton the Templars owned a house with outbuildings, 100 acres of arable land and a pasture. Wulfstan or Wulstan had been a Benedictine monk at Worcester Cathedral Priory and in 1062 he became the new Bishop of Worcester. His ready submission to William the Conqueror in 1066 and his reputation for holiness made him one of the few Englishmen to retain high office under the Normans and when he died in 1095 he was the last English bishop in the Norman Church. The late 13th-century church at Welsh Newton was appropriated to the Templars because in the then custodian John de la Haye's accounts of 1313 he 'answers for 106s. 8d. received of tithes of Newtone's church'. No expenses for a priest were recorded but this could mean that one of the Templars' own chaplains was taking the services, which they were allowed to do. John de la Haye records that rents were collected; fruit was sold; 3s. came from the Dovecot; workers were paid and roofs were repaired. Today the only evidence of the Templar property is in the name shared by a wood and a farm, St. Wolstan, built in the 16th century.

Rowlestone was a small estate, with a manor house and 200 acres, which was rented out. In 1338 a bailiff, who was paid £1 10s. by Dinmore (when the property had been passed to the Hospitallers), collected 13s. 4d. from the court, £3 0s. 10½d. in rents and £5 from 200 acres of arable land. This was probably the present Court farm which dates back to the 14th century.

In Harewood the Templars had a manor house, a watermill, 200 acres of arable land, a pasture and an appropriated church. Rees tells that this estate was formerly granted by King John to Godscall (Godescallus) who transferred it to the Templars at Garway. But maybe John gave it directly to the Templars as in a document dated 21 August 1215, 'The King to the Sheriff of Hereford. Know ye that for God we confer and by our charter confirm to the Master and Brethren of the Knights of the Temple in England all our land in Harwood'. In 1313 John de la Haye notes that rents had been collected; there was no profit from the mill as it was broken down; fruit from the garden had been sold; repairs had been made to the wall of the Hall at Harewood, and the roofs of several houses and that workmen had been paid. A chaplain for Harewood Church had been paid 6s. 8d. for the year while donations of 6d., and the monetary value of the tithes 3s., had been received. After the Dissolution of the Monasteries a house was built on the site and Harewood Park made a superb home for successive owners until its demolition in 1959. In 1981 a modern window depicting Hospitallers was removed from the 18th-century chapel to Coningsby Hospital.

William Marshall, Earl of Pembroke, was a loyal servant of the Crown for almost 50 years, being made Regent during the boyhood of King Henry III. Shortly before he died William Marshall became a Knight of the Temple and in 1219 was buried with great pomp before the high altar of the Temple Church in London. Rees names Marshall as the donor of the gift of 4 hides (a hide could vary between 60 and 180 acres), at Upleadon, in the Parish of Bosbury. Today the only clue to the presence of the Templars here is in the name of Temple Court Farm. The Report of 1338 records a manor house with a garden, a dovecote, a watermill, 740 acres of land, 40 acres of meadow and several pastures. Altogether, with rents and court fines the estate was worth £44 4s. 8d. The expenses for the household totalled £15 12s. Corn for bread making cost £3; malted corn and rye for brewing £3 5s.; for the kitchen £3; wine, wax and oil for the chapel 3s. 8d.; for the chaplain £1; Ricardi Pauely, a corrodary working in the chapel, was paid 10s.—could he be a relation of Gilbert Pauely of Dinmore?; the bailiff received 13s. 4d.; as did the cook; the prior's visit for two days cost £2; various rents amounted to 6s. 8d.; payment for the work of the seneschal in the courts £1. The Hospitaller accounts indicate a busy and well organised house, which surely reflects the previous ownership of the Templars.

In 1491, six years after William Bongam had successfully claimed sanctuary at Wormbridge, Philip Baret a tailor of Upleadon claimed sanctuary at

‘Templecourt’ after killing John Berne. He was forcibly removed and taken to the king’s goal at Hereford. Representing the Hospitallers Thomas Leyland stated that Templecourt was part of the Preceptory of Dinmore and requested that Baret be returned there to remain ‘safe and secure there for as long as he pleases’. The Law of Sanctuary prevailed and the Sheriff was ordered to return Baret there in safety under a penalty of £100.

In Hereford there is a suggestion of a short-lived Templar presence at St. Giles’s Hospital. Consisting of a chapel and tenements, St. Giles’s Hospital was founded in the 12th century on the north-east side of St. Owens Street, outside the line of the city walls. The chapel was rebuilt in 1682, but demolished in 1927 in order to widen the road. During the demolition the foundations of the 12th-century chapel were discovered, revealing it to have been circular, intimating that it may have had Templar origins. It measured just under 27 feet in internal diameter with walls 3 feet 6 inches thick. There was evidence that the walls had been plastered, but none for any arcading or pilasters. There were also indications of an apsidal chancel to the east. Nothing appears to be known as to the chapel’s or hospital’s origins, but it is

The round nave of the putative Templar chapel at St. Giles’s Chapel, Hereford, when excavated in 1927

believed that it was soon abandoned by the Templars and subsequently taken over by the Dominicans or Black Friars when they first came to Hereford in 1246. This was strongly resisted by the city clergy and Bishop Cantilupe ordered them to leave the site for a better one given to them at Widemarsh. The first documentary record of the place comes on 29 November 1321, when Bishop Adam de Orleton commissioned Master R. de Vernon to settle Alice, daughter of Roger de Atforton, as an anchoress at the 'Church of St. Giles in a suburb of Hereford'. She presumably took over the decaying chapel and when she died or left, it passed to the king who in turn passed it to the city corporation for use as an almshouse. Interestingly, the almshouse constitution was modelled on that of the Templars, with the positions of a custos and chaplain. In confirming the grant in 1392, Richard II referred to the 'Custos and Mendicants of St. Giles'. The chapel survived to at least the time of the map-maker Speed, for his map of 1610 shows the round chapel with a domed roof and chancel attached. Taylor's map of 1752 shows a small building abutting the northern side of the rebuilt chapel; this was probably the chaplain's house.[10]

The weather-worn tympanum from St. Giles's Chapel depicting Christ in Majesty/Ascension

A plaster cast made of the capital from St. Giles's chapel, believed to depict Christ the Good Shepherd

A mid to late 12th-century tympanum is now built into the east wall of the Williams almshouses nearby, along with a much weather-beaten double capital and grotesque corbel. The origins of these had been a puzzle until the foundations of the chapel were discovered in 1927. The carvings are closely related to work of the Herefordshire School at Shobdon, indicating that the chapel might have been built in the 1130s. Just as there is slight mystery over the Hospitaller presence at Coningsby Hospital, so is there over any Templar connection with St. Giles's Hospital.

We are on much firmer ground when considering Garway. The *Book of Llandaff* contains entries which experts have agreed refer to land in Garway in the early part of the 6th century. One records that the King of Archenfield gave an uncia of land, 108 acres, 'for the sake of the heavenly kingdom unto God' and St. Dubricius and his community. It then describes the consecration of the land and lists the dignitaries who witnessed the ceremony, among whom were Bishop Uvelviu, David the chief priest, King Gurvodu of Archenfield and his son Ervic. The bishop 'walking around the piece of land, with the holy cross going on before, with the holy relics, and with the sprinkling of holy water in the midst, founded the place in honour of the Holy Trinity; and placed there Guorvoe his priest, and commended the place to him, to serve for the permanent use of a church.' The church would have been an integral part of a Welsh settlement of monastic buildings known as a *Clas* which was home to a group of peripatetic missionary monks and their families. The monks' purpose was to spread the word of Jesus to the people in the surrounding countryside. Close to St. Michaels Church at Garway is a field named 'Old Lands', the name suggesting an area of early cultivation, perhaps when the land was first worked to provide food for this *Clas* community. An essential requirement for the *Clas* was water, and running water can still be found in the south-east corner of Garway churchyard.

Herman's castellry referred to in Richard I's charter of 1189 was presumably established in support of the Norman castle in Ewyas Harold. The existence of the castellry indicates that Garway also had a church and it is reasonable to assume that the Normans made use of the *Clas* site, as did the Templars subsequently for their preceptory.

The position and layout of the Templar preceptory at Garway can only be estimated from the clues left behind as it was not a monastery in the accepted sense, where a brotherhood of monks would devote their lives to prayer.

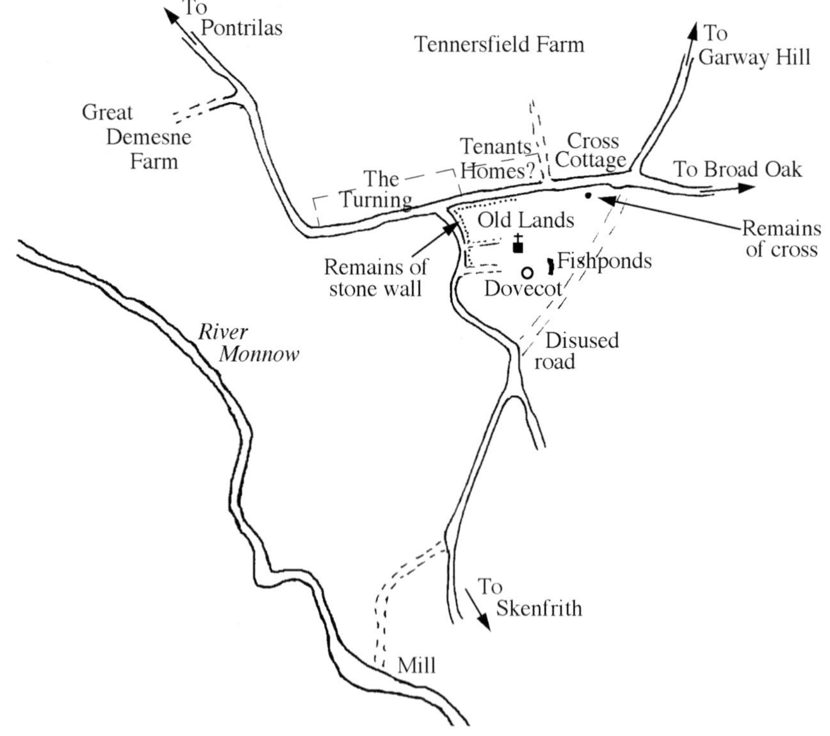

Plan of the area around Garway church showing places mentioned in the text

Remains of a medieval limekiln found in a field near the church

Instead the Templars' main task was to make a profit from their land, yet, as they belonged to a religious order, the buildings and the positions they occupied would nevertheless be similar to those of a monastery. Even after almost 900 years there is considerable evidence to prove this. The remains of a stone wall, which could have been the preceptory wall, can still be found in the base of the roadside hedge which bounds fields south of the road, including 'Old Lands', and runs from opposite the drive to Tennersfield Farm west as far as The Turning.

Some years ago, on one of the rare occasions when Old Lands had been ploughed, Dave Jemmett of Monmouth Archaeological Society was given permission to walk the field. He found evidence of two large rectangular buildings and some medieval roof tile fragments, which he took to be archaeological evidence of Templar barns. During an exploratory excavation in the adjacent field he discovered remains of a wall on the western boundary of the field continuing south from The Turning down to the Church Farm gateway.

Until the 1960s, when the new Church Road was created allowing access to the church, the main entrance to Church Farm was just south of its present entrance. Sited in the west wall this would have been the ideal position for the main entrance to the preceptory. In the same field Jemmett uncovered the superb remains of a medieval limekiln, and the foundations of several buildings. The kiln was the first one of its kind to have been found in Herefordshire, and one of only 50 discovered in the whole country. Lime was an essential ingredient in the making of medieval mortar and this limekiln must surely have been used in Templar or Hospitaller buildings, or even both.

Cressing Temple in Essex was given to the Templars by Queen Mathilda in 1137, and in 1987 the medieval farm complex there was acquired by Essex County Council. Their main objective was 'the development of the site as one of the focal points for the historic heritage of Essex, based upon the preservation of its historical and archaeological value'. The 'Great Barns' there have been restored and today appear just as they did in the 13th century. The Barley Barn, which is dated 1200–1220, is 120 feet long and 48 feet wide and the Wheat Barn, dated around 1260, is 130 feet long and 44 feet wide. Today we tend to call all large farm buildings 'barns' but the medieval barn was purpose built specifically for the corn harvest. The barns in Garway, which had also been built by Templars, were probably very similar to those now seen at Cressing Temple.

A house in Garway called Cross Cottage lies on the opposite side of the road to a small triangle of common land on which stands the base of an ancient cross. It would be reasonable to expect the roads to cross at this point and not to meet in a T-junction as they do now. In the meadow to the south obvious tracks lead straight down from the junction to meet with the road to Skenfrith, which suggests that at one time the roads did cross. If this was the case then the road leading south from The Turning to Skenfrith was purpose built to give access to the Preceptory gatehouse. Over the centuries this subsidiary road became the main road to Skenfrith and the crossroads became a junction. The southern section of the original north-south road then fell into disuse but has not yet completely disappeared. There is another possibility. When the new preceptory was completed the easternmost buildings were very close to the road, perhaps it was forced out of use rather than disused, to sustain the Templars' privacy. All travellers would then have to go by way of the new road up to, and down from, The Turning.

Five hundred years after the suppression of the Order of the Temple of Solomon the 1841 Tithe Map records that 99 acres 2 rods 11 perches of

William Embry's land, which had once belonged to the Templars, were still exempt from tithe. The fields that were specified as 'No tithe – Free by prescription' were grouped around the Tennersfield farmhouse. In an aerial photograph taken by Cambridge University Committee for Aerial Photography in 1966, an area just south of the farmhouse and north of Garway Church was assessed as a deserted medieval village. The villagers of Garway, like the inhabitants of all medieval manors, were a mixture of skilled workers and labourers all of whom were tenants of the local lord. Carpenters, blacksmiths, millers, herdsmen, and all those others who could provide essential services, were able to earn enough to rent their own homes and a small parcel of land. Those who had nothing but labouring to offer were committed to a number of set days every week when they worked their lord's demesne in

The Cambridge Committee for Aerial Photography's photograph of Garway, showing the church in the foreground and the site of the deserted medieval village above it, to the north

Aerial view of Garway church and Church Farm

order to have a home. (There is a farm in the Monnow Valley just west of Garway that is called Demesne and may, therefore, have formed part of the property.) At certain times of the year such as harvest, everyone was expected to help and was paid for the extra work. The tenants grew their own food, kept their own livestock and lived closely together on the tenants' field. In the 10th century *feld*, an Old English word meaning open country, came to mean arable land that had been recently cleared, and not our modern meaning of an area of land usually bounded by fences. Tenants' field easily becomes tenors field when spoken casually and it is feasible that 'Tennersfield' Farm was so named because it developed around the land that once housed the villagers who were Templar tenants. It seems pretty conclusive that the villagers working for the Templars lived just across the road from the preceptory.

The Columbarium is on the far left

The water that had attracted the missionaries of the *Clas* to the site in the 6th century would have been equally important to 12th-century Templars for their cooking, cleaning and drainage needs, and even for keeping the fish-ponds full. It continued as an important source of fresh water for the villagers of Garway until mains water was provided in the 20th century. The Norman Lords of the manor built mills and then forbade the use of personal querns, which the local people had always used to grind their corn, compelling the villagers to pay for the privilege of having their grain ground for them. The river Monnow would have provided a convenient source of power for the watermill and S.D. Coates and D.G. Tucker write that 'there are remains of a mill on the Monnow at Garway, and evidence that there was a corn mill at Garway in the 14th and 16th centuries'.[11] One of the Garway families must have hidden a quern in the hope of better times to come, as one was found when a grave was being dug in the churchyard.

The king's permission to build a dovecote, or *columbarium*, was a privilege accorded only to barons, lords of the manor and monasteries. Dovecotes and fishponds were usually close to the domestic buildings, maybe for convenience or perhaps to deter poachers. The Templars had such a dovecote and in the triangular tympanum over the south doorway are traces of an inscription carved in Lombardic capitals which was recorded before it weathered beyond redemption and translates as, 'In the year of Our Lord 1326 this dove-cote was made by Brother Richard de Biri'. A tympanum was an architectural feature not generally seen after 1300, yet de la Haye's accounts of 1313 indicate that the dovecote of the Templars was broken down. It is hard to say, therefore, if Brother Richard repaired the original or built a completely new one. Whether Templar or Hospitaller, the dovecote in Garway is regarded as the best example of a medieval *columbarium* in England. It is a circular building sited south-east of the church with an internal diameter of 17 feet 6 inches and walls 3 feet 10 inches thick. Arranged around the interior walls, in 19 rows, are

The interior of the columbarium *from an old postcard*

666 L-shaped nesting spaces with landing ledges, each large enough for two parent birds and two chicks. A small rounded cupola, which can best be seen from the north-east corner of the churchyard, not only embellished the dovecote but protected the interior from rain. It also allowed the birds freedom to fly in and out and could be manually controlled when necessary. The rock pigeons that were kept were highly prolific and provided a welcome source of food throughout the year. Eggs were obviously used but so too were the young birds, known as squabs and squeakers, which were especially delectable. In addition there were useful by-products. Feathers and down were collected to fill pillows and feather mattresses, and the guano produced was used to enrich the soil or to soften leather in the tanning process. Eggs and the young, at four weeks old, were collected by means of a potence. This was a central post, secured by one pivot into a roof beam and by another into the centre of the floor, with arms extended from the post to carry ladders close to the walls. The potence was so well balanced that it could be turned by the touch of a finger which made all nests accessible to the collector who was able to move to the left and right by pulling on the holes and ledges, and up and down using the ladder, The dovecote owners were well satisfied with the arrangements, but not so the tenants whose crops grew close by. It could be that the tenants' hatred of these birds had resulted in damage to the *columbarium* sometime between the departure of the Templars and the arrival of the Hospitallers.

The two fishponds of the preceptory are just east of the dovecote but have been modified over the years by various owners of Church Farm.

In the garden wall south of the church are four beeboles, purpose-built recesses made in the wall as it was built, which supported and protected individual woven wicker bee hives called skeps. It is possible that these were made and used by the Templars. 'Medieval records in general indicate that the great importance of beeswax was its use for candles in the Christian church, and some even suggest that the primary purpose of beekeeping was to provide candles for mass'.[12]

During their time in Garway the Templars and their tenants brought into use 720 acres of arable land and 60 acres of meadow.

When Edward II ordered the imprisonment of the English Knights of the Temple in 1308, there were 135 Templars based in England, including 6 knights and 11 priests. Among them were two brothers from Garway: Philip de Mewes, the Preceptor of Garway, and William Pokelington. A confession by John Stoke, who came to Garway about 1294 after having been in the

Beeboles at Church House for holding wicker beehives, or skeps. The nave walls of the church are in the background

Order for a year, is retold in the notes of St. John's Historical Society who visited Hereford in June 1985:

> He was lame and therefore not allowed to become a member of Chapter (presumably he would be unable to fight if the need arose), and he had been Treasurer of the Temple in London. He was in Garway during the visit there by Grand Master Jacques de Molay. Stoke's deposition when the Templars were arrested, was that he had been called to the Grand Master's bedchamber at Garway and in front of two other foreign knights he was asked to make proof of his obedience, and to seat himself on a small stool at the foot of the Grand Master's bed. De Molay then sent to the Church for a crucifix and the two other Templars placed themselves at either side of the door with their swords drawn. Stoke said that he was asked to deny 'Him whom the image represents', but he replied 'Far be it for me to deny my Saviour'. The Grand Master ordered him to do so, otherwise he would be put in a sack and carried to a place 'by no means agreeable'. Through fear of death he denied Christ, 'but with his tongue and not his heart'. Though the Templars

were not tortured in England as they were in France it is possible that John Stoke's 'fear of death' also caused him to denounce his Grand Master with his tongue.

Despite such testimony, by 1310 examination of the English Templars had found no substance to the accusations against them and they were allowed to join another monastic order, but not the Hospitallers, or to return to the secular life.

King Edward II followed the pope's instruction to take possession of the Templar property, but not for the pope's benefit. Instead he sold their wool, used stores of grain for his war against Scotland, drew on Templar reserves of meat and fish for his coronation feast on 25th February 1308, and used Templar funds to pay arrears to his clerks, and provide alms for religious houses. He stripped estates of horses and stock, kitchen equipment and any other moveable property even stripping the lands of their timber.[13]

By 1311 the Templar property at Garway was held by Sir Richard Harley, presumably illegally, for

> On November 14th 1326 Philip, Rector of Rushbury, in Shropshire was commissioned to absolve the Lady Burga, widow of Richard de Harley, from the excommunication and interdict pronounced against those who had illicitly occupied and held lands formerly belonging to the Military Order of the Temple, since she had made satisfaction to Richard de Payeley, Preceptor of Dinmore. The Lady Burga, or her late husband, was doubtless among those who had either been granted a Templar property by the King, or had entered upon lands given to the Templars by an ancestor.[14]

Nevertheless, in 1311 the property was held by Harley under the custody of John de la Haye. His annual account for 1313 provides an interesting insight into the running of the property. During the year £4 6s. had been received from the courts, Garway mill had taken 65s. but had needed 10d. worth of iron and steel, presumably for repairs, and a new millstone which had cost 5s. There was no profit from the dovecote because it was broken down. Live animals, oxen, cows, sheep and pigs were sold and so were the hides of dead ones—an ox, 2 cows and a calf. Corn, hay, beans and fruit had been harvested and sold. Sheep were being kept, ointment had been bought for them and milk had been bought for the lambs, lights were bought for watching the sheep and lambs, expenses had been paid for shearing and the wool had been sold. Milk was sold and so was cheese. An interesting item in the accounts is of linen cloth bought for wrapping the cheeses when they were made, the linen possibly being spun and woven by Templar tenants from flax grown in the village. Salt was purchased for the dairy and the household; white leather was bought for making and repairing various harnesses; two bags for carrying seed into the fields and two new fans for winnowing had also been bought that year. The roofs of several houses had been repaired, some in stone and some with thatch. In the autumn a carter had been paid 3s. for collecting and carrying the church tithes, the boy who helped him was paid 20d.

The Church expenses listed in the accounts also indicate the uninterrupted work of Garway church during the unsettled time after the arrest of the Templars. £2 9s. 6d. was received and the clerk serving the church received 5s. and 4qrs. 2½bz (?Bushels) of wheat. Items purchased included wine for Mass and Easter at 13d.; four pounds of wax to make candles for Christmas and Easter at 3s.; oil for the lamps at 6d. and incense at 2d.

Also listed in de la Haye's accounts was David of Lancleudy, a chaplain who received wages at 3d. a day. Three other men, Robert de Newebotel, Gilbert de Penebrugge and William de Egle were included, 'with the latter's gowns and shoes'. Maybe these three had been Templar corrodaries and were living in the house awaiting the arrival of the Hospitallers in anticipation of continued security. Presumably the Hospitallers accepted the responsibility of all the Templar corrodaries along with inheritance of the properties.

Twenty-five years later The Hospitaller Report of 1338 has a section for Garway which gives a clear picture of the life of the Hospitallers there. Their profits for the year amounted to £87 0s. 4d., most of which came from renting out land. The care of travellers, especially the sick and needy, continued to be of great importance to the Hospitallers and much of Garway's income was used in providing for visitors, 'of whom many [came] from Wales'. Amongst the purchases were 60qrs. of corn for making bread which would have yielded 51 pounds of bread a week, and 20qrs. of brewing corn and 80qrs. of brewing oats for making 180 gallons of ale a week. Meat, fish and other requisites for the kitchen were purchased and a chamberlain, two pages, a cook, a porter and a baker were among the servants employed. As well as visitors there were three holders of corrodies at Garway at this time, Guilbert of Pembroke who received £1 a year and ate at the table of the brothers, and Hugh Despenser and Stephen Port who each received 10 shillings a year and ate at the table of the free servants. After settling their accounts, the Hospitallers at Garway 'sent to the Treasury for bearing burdens £40 3s. 4d.' With only one church in the village, the monastic brothers and the local people worshipped in the same building, the lay parishioners in the nave, with the monks and the officiating priests in the chancel. It was an appropriated church from which £10 was collected, the chaplain, who was provided with two pages, was paid £1 a year for celebrating mass and a total of 6s. 8d was spent on wine, wax for making candles, and oil for the lamps that lit the church.

At the beginning of the 16th century John ap Phillpott rented land in Garway from the Hospitallers. He was to pay ten shillings on 24 June, the Feast of the Nativity of St. John the Baptist, and ten shillings on 2 February, the Purification of the Virgin Mary. The land rented was described as Tenors Field lying between a field of St. Magdalen and the Oldfield, and a meadow called Long Meadow. Tenors Field conforms exactly to the Templars' Tenants' field, which in William Embry's time was exempt from tithe,

Although the Knights Hospitaller were at Garway for 200 years there is little information about their time there. By the beginning of the 16th century much of the land had been leased to Richard Mynors and Thomas ap Lea of Garway. On 1st July 1512 the lease to Sir Richard Mynors and his son Roger was renewed for 21 years. They were to find a chaplain for the services of the church and the cure of the parishioners. It was stated that the edifices though well built, nevertheless were not kept in proper repair and were ruinous. The following buildings are enumerated: one chancel with a chapel annexed, presumably in good condition, as nothing is said under this head; one *columbarium* well and sufficiently repaired; a hall ruinous and almost fallen to the ground; a parlour and a room annexed very ruinous and similarly almost fallen to the ground; a stable with a room called the Priest's chamber, very ruinous through neglect of repairs both to the timber work and the roof covering; a barn near the pigeon house very ruinous; a house called a 'cowheus' situated near the cemetery of the church, very ruinous and almost fallen to the ground; and a water mill with a stone stank, namely the weir of the said mill, very ruinous both in respect of the timber work as well as the stone work. From the above it is evident that the buildings in 1512 were in a hopelessly neglected condition and uninhabitable.[15]

At the Dissolution the huge areas of land that had previously been owned by the monasteries became available to those wealthy enough to purchase them. In many cases the land had already been rented out for a long time and lessees with sufficient capital were quick to become landowners. The Hospitaller estate at Garway was no exception, when inspectors from RCHM visited Garway they dated three farmhouses and two barns as having been built in the late 16th century or early 17th century.

St. Michael's Church, Garway

St. Michael's Church is not only the largest and most ancient building in Garway, it is a treasure-house of history. For almost 900 years it has continued to provide a place of worship for the local people. Long before the advent of Parish Halls the medieval village church was the only convenient meeting place for the parishioners and all public events such as manorial courts, sports, village fairs and Church Ales were held in the church or the churchyard. Three clear building phases have been identified: the original Templar construction, the alterations and improvements made by the Hospitallers, and modifications made in the aftermath of the Reformation. The earlier *Clas* church would have been of timber and all traces have been lost.

Garway Church and tower

The church is built of sandstone rubble and dressings, with some use of tufa. The round nave, perhaps with an apsidal east end, was built in the last quarter of the 12th century, the detached tower being added in the early 13th century. Later still the chancel was extended to the east, and a south chapel

The chancel arch at Garway

Waterleaf and grotesque capitals of the chancel arch

added. The nave was rebuilt on a rectangular plan in the 14th century. The north wall of the chancel contains three windows dating from *c*.1250, the same date attributed to the middle window of the east wall, which contains three re-set windows. In the south wall is an arcade of the same date. The semi-circular chancel arch is dated earlier, to 1175–80. This is plain on the east side, facing the chancel, but richly decorated on the west where it marks the break between the nave and the part of the church used by the clergy. The west face of the arch has three orders, the outer carved with chevrons, the middle with an interlacing chevron pattern and the inner carved on the side facing into the arch. The outer two orders are carried on capitals carved with waterleaf, except for the inner shaft on the north side which has a grotesque head. The chancel arch's chevron mouldings are typical of the Norman period while other details such as the transverse mouldings carved on the inner order of the arch across each voussoir, the wedge-shaped stones that form the arch, are unusual. Anderson mentions a similar arch at Winchfield in Hampshire which 'may have been copied from the decoration of the Bab-el-Foutouh at Cairo built in 1090'. In his *Buildings of England, Herefordshire*, Nikolaus Pevsner describes the waterleaf capital, the top part of a column, as rare in Herefordshire and found only in Abbey Dore, Cleonger, Kings Pyon and Garway. The waterleaf decoration was very common in Cistercian churches but its use in Britain was confined to the years between 1165 and 1190.[16]

In 1927, Mr. Gavin H. Jack, the County Surveyor for Herefordshire, carried out an excavation in which the circular nave was rediscovered. His account noted that: 'The foundations of local unsquared sandstone were laid

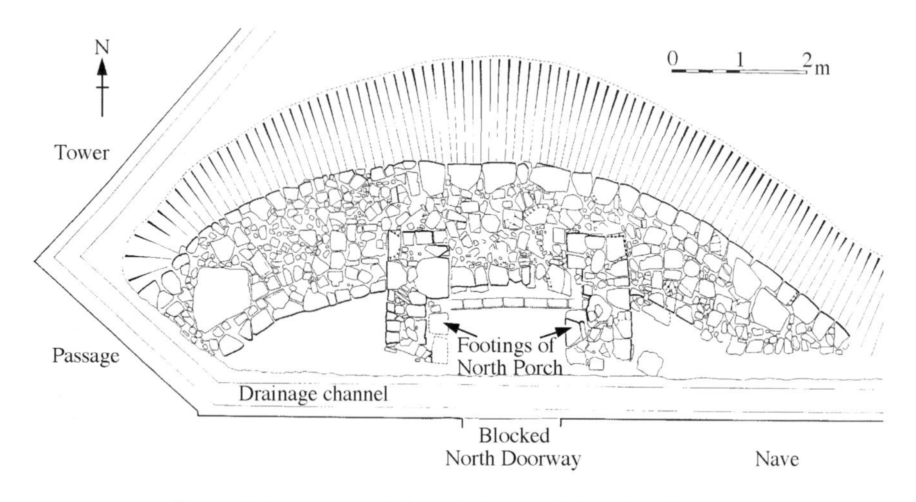

Plan of the exposed foundations of the circular nave on the north side of Garway church

in good mortar and were about 2ft. 6in. in depth and 5ft. 8in. wide. On these the circular wall of the church, about 3ft. 6in. thick, was built. The internal diameter of the circular nave was 43ft. 9in. During the excavations one fragment of twelfth-century moulding was found and two fragments of other worked stone, possibly parts of a stone coffin. Lying on top of the foundations I found the top of a two-branch iron candlestick much corroded. Several fragments of red pottery showing medieval glaze were found. Unfortunately I had insufficient time (and money) to search for the remains of a porch at the west end, or to make any attempt at excavating the site of the preceptory buildings, remains of which undoubtedly exist on the south side of the church'.[17]

Although the dig in the south was backfilled, remains of the Templars' round nave on the north side of the church have been preserved and protected. Further evidence can be seen inside the nave in the south-east corner above the Roll of Honour, where a ledge clearly reveals part of the curved wall of the circular nave, whilst the corresponding north-east 'corner' is just that, a perfect corner. Maybe this was not just an oversight, when planning the building of the rectangular nave, but a deliberate action on somebody's part in order to keep one small piece of evidence for future generations to recognise. Garway now has the only visible and accessible remains of a circular nave of a Templar church to be seen in Britain.

The 70 foot high tower was built by the Templars. Originally detached from the church it is thought to have been a place of refuge for the villagers

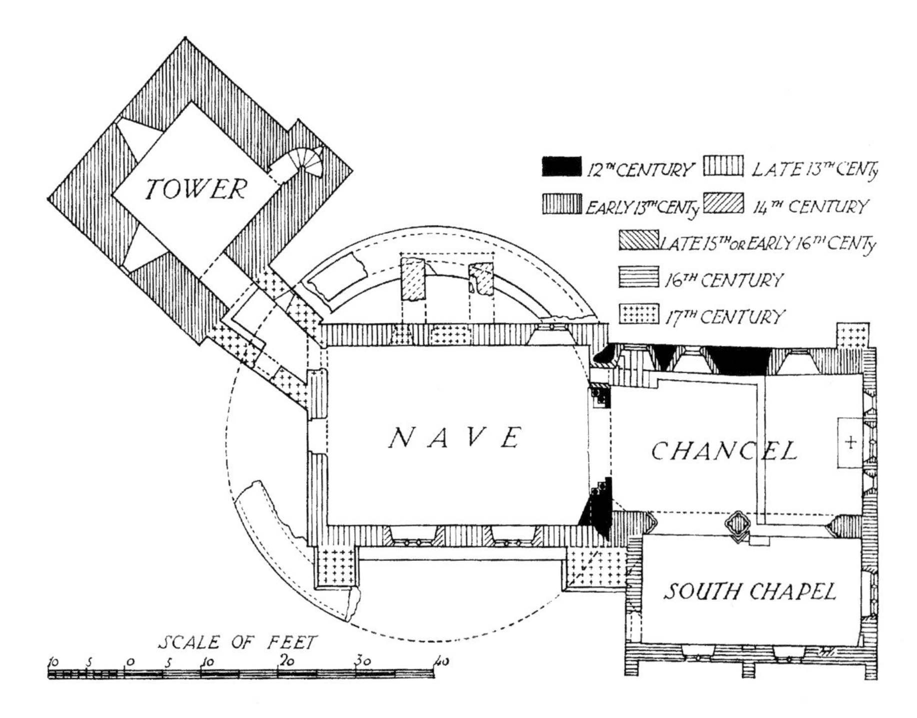

Plan of the church from the 1932 Royal Commission report

during the troubled periods of history in the Welsh Marches. Its three floors are linked by a circular stone staircase or 'vice' (from the French *vis*, 'screw') in the north-west corner which is contained in the projection seen in the exterior north wall. In the interior east wall is a small hole about 7 inches square, which once passed right through the thick tower wall until it was later blocked in the exterior wall. Many ideas as to its use have been proffered including being a means of passing food through to prisoners held in the tower. It is possible that, when the church had a round nave, it was a type of 'squint', allowing a view of the altar so that the bell ringers would know exactly when to ring, for example at the elevation of the host during the service of Mass.

Originally 8 feet shorter, the development of complicated change ringing in the 16th century was probably the reason why the tower was heightened. The same reason can be used to explain the need for the passageway that still provides shelter for the team of bellringers between the tower and the church. It was made from reused material including tufa the large distinctive pieces of stone full of holes. Tufa is found locally in limestone areas and occurs where water springs from the ground when it evaporates leaving limestone deposits

The 12th-century chest

which precipitate around vegetation, sticks or stones. Although soft at first it hardens without becoming heavy and makes an ideal building material, especially when working high up, that was well used by the Normans in Herefordshire.

Now kept in the tower is a wonderful 12th-century dug-out trunk. In 1199, seeking funds for the Fourth Crusade, the pope asked that a trunk should be placed in every church in which all the faithful should place alms for the remission of their sins.[18] The chest was to be kept locked with three keys, one to be kept by the bishop, one by the priest of the church and one by a devout layman. A bull of 1213 was similarly worded and concluded that the 'alms for the Holy Land in this chest is to be spent according to the decision of those to whom this concern is entrusted'. It is thought that Garway's chest was made by local craftsmen as a result of these papal bulls.

The cemetery, north of the church, is considerably higher than the floor level of the church, a fact that many visitors question. This is often due to the use of ground for burials over the centuries, and if the church of St. Michael Super Mingui during the reign of Edward the Confessor was on the same site, then numerous burials over a 1,000 year period may explain the difference in soil levels. If the same site had been used since the *Clas* of the 6th century the time span could be 1,500 years.

The Hospitallers arrived to take possession of the Garway property around 1326, and the RCHM dates the rectangular nave to the early 14th century. Presumably it was in the time of the Hospitallers that the new nave was built.

There were no seats for the medieval congregation. The parishioners who came to worship in the church stood or knelt on the earth floor of the nave that would have been strewn with rushes, herbs or hedgerow plants. A stone ledge set against the wall for the elderly and infirm to use is said to have given rise to the saying 'let the weak go the wall'. The oak benches used today are the original seats that date from the 16th century. The 14th-century font of the Hospitallers is still being used and may even be standing in the same position as it did over 600 years ago, equidistant from the north and west doorways.

On the exterior north wall of the nave a blocked doorway and signs of a porch roof can be easily identified. This was the door that was regularly used by the congregation, as the Order's domestic buildings were south of the church. The porch was the place where marriage banns were announced, the first part of the marriage ceremony performed before the bride and groom entered the church together, and women were not allowed into church after giving birth until they had been 'churched' in a ceremony that took place in the porch. The first part of the baptismal service was also held there, after which the priest escorted those involved into the church where they gathered around the font, which was always situated close to the door. The porch was the most suitable place for the signing of documents, the settling of debts and other business matters as there were always plenty of witnesses available. It was also where a fugitive claiming sanctuary confessed his crime before leaving the country. With the introduction of the Protestant Faith the porch lost its importance, which is when it was probably dismantled and the north doorway blocked up. The west doorway that originally had been used only for ceremonial purposes, when processions proceeded all around the interior and exterior of the church, then became the main entry into the church.

Although a new nave was built the chancel arch built by the Templars was not replaced. A decorated screen would have stretched across the width of the arch with a 'rood' above it. The rood was the wooden carving of Christ crucified with the companion figures of the Virgin Mary and St. John the Evangelist. Rood stairs gave access for the lighting of candles around the rood and for its decoration on important dates in the church calendar. The screen's purpose was to separate the congregation in the nave from the religious ritual in the chancel. Its central doorway was closed and secured when the service was over ensuring the inaccessibility, and reinforcing the mystery, of the altar. As in many other churches the rood and the screen were destroyed during the change from the Catholic to the Protestant faith.

In the many phases of rebuilding, Templar coffin lids have been widely reused, one can be seen in the centre of the chancel step, there are others in the rood stair, the altar step, and in the lintels of windows in the south chapel and in the tower passage.

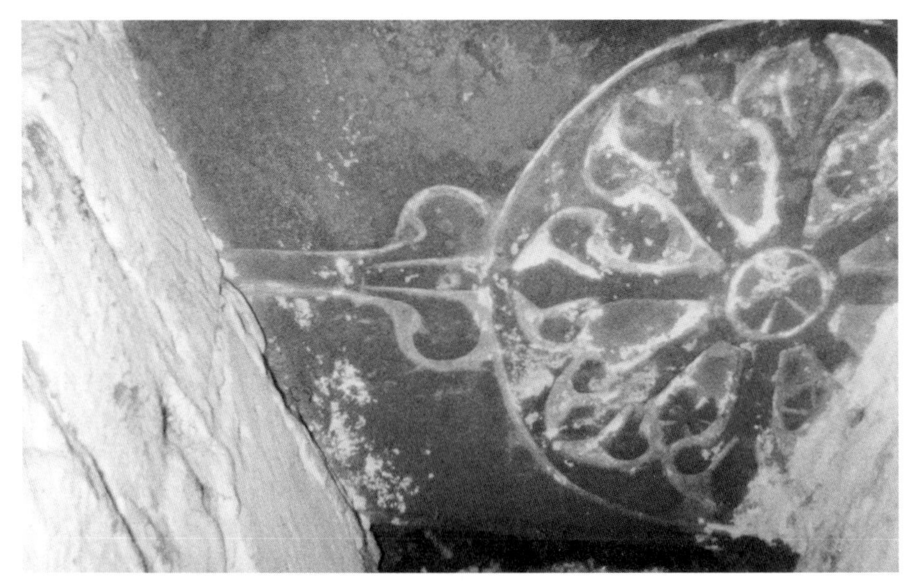

Templar coffin lid re-used as a window lintel in the passage to the tower

The 13th-century Templar window in the north-west corner of the chancel was partly blocked by the Hospitallers in order to build steps up to the rood loft. It was then necessary to make a doorway in the chancel wall to give access to the rood. In the south-west corner of the chancel is a huge block of masonry which seems to have no visible purpose. But George Marshall told the Woolhope Club on 29th September 1927 that 'part of this block was built undoubtedly as a vice, which, if an entry could be effected, might still be found within.' He also referred to a description given by the Rev. M.G. Watkins writing in 1900, that 'a heavy stone staircase on the left of the chancel leads to the rood loft. Another on the right is blocked by monuments'.[19] These comments infer that at some stage the staircase had been observed. The Hospitallers must have had a very good reason for building a new rood stair to replace the vice built by the Templars. At Temple Bruer, a Templar property in Lincolnshire, there was a similar block of masonry in the same position with steps down to a crypt and evidence of a newel staircase leading upwards. George Marshall said it was impossible to identify the entrance to the vice in Garway—it could be from the east wall of the nave or the west wall of the chapel or perhaps more likely from outside the building, but evidently not from the chancel. Could it be that in Garway the vice was the night stair leading from the Templars' dorter into the south chapel or the chancel, and also provided access to the rood loft. There is a suggestion of a blocked entrance in the exterior of the south wall that would correspond with the top of the vice.

The chancel roof was hidden until the early 1900s, when a 15th-century roof built by the Hospitallers was revealed. The RCHM described it so: 'It is in three main bays, each sub-divided. The main trusses have big stopped chamfered tie beams; king posts, collars and braces to the principals. The subsidiary trusses have braces to the collars, forming segmental arches'. This description fits perfectly with details given by Pevsner of the typical 15th-century Herefordshire roof used in both churches and houses.[20]

There is only one item in the chancel that can be clearly identified with the Templars—the altar stone. Hidden in the floor at the time of the Reformation, when it was ordered that altar stones were to be destroyed and replaced with wooden tables, it was recognised in 1872 by Rev. Charles J. Robinson. In his book *Mansions and Manors of Herefordshire* he wrote of 'the old altar stone now part of the chancel pavement'. Six years later it was taken out of the floor where it had lain for more than 300 years and set on an oak frame, finally in 1967 it was placed onto pillars of Bath Stone. There are five crosses carved in the altar, one at each corner and one in the centre, which represent the Five Wounds of Christ. These would have been filled with oil in an act of consecration before the altar stone could be used as the Lord's table.

Although the south chapel has an arcade with the pointed arches of the Early English architectural period of the 13th century, the chapel itself was part of the original 12th-century Templar building. There has been a lot of rebuilding here and few objects have been positively dated. In the southern corner of the east wall is a recess, the remains of an aumbry which was a cupboard for the sacred vessels used in church services. Close by in the south wall is a piscina where those same chalices and patens were washed. It was very important that water that had been in contact with consecrated bread and wine should not be allowed to touch unhallowed ground and piscina drains always led directly under the church buildings. The stone surround of the piscina has a number of carvings, a chalice, a round wafer, a fish and an eel-like creature. The reason for the chalice and wafer are obvious and the fish often depicts Christ as the letters of the Greek word for fish are the initial letters of Jesus Son of God Saviour, but the eel-like creature has so far escaped identification.

In the mid-20th century when repairs to the church were being carried out, a large collection of bones was found under the floor of the south chapel. A difficult decision had to be made! The weather was atrocious, there had been heavy falls of snow and a wedding was arranged for the end of the week. If discovery of the bones was reported the floor could not be replaced until an investigation had taken place. But experts would not be able to get out to Garway until the weather improved and that would mean that the wedding would have to be postponed. It was decided to carry on with the repairs, the floor was relaid and the wedding took place. Coffins were not used for all burials until the 19th century, until then the corpse was buried in a shroud and only put into the parish coffin for the funeral journey to the church. After a period of time the bones could easily be identified, retrieved and put into an ossuary, bone-hole or charnel house.

Over the west door in the south chapel emblems of Christ's Passion have been incised. They have gradually become more difficult to identify but the spear, ladder, three nails, a Tau cross with a crown, a sword, a sponge on a reed and a cup and with a cover can still be made out.

All around the exterior walls of the church are interesting features that have given the experts problems in identifying and dating, including various crosses and possible masons' marks. High up above the west door of the nave is a winged dragon or wyvern. In the Public Record Office is a Templar manuscript with griffins and wyverns decorating its leather cover. As most of the medieval congregation were illiterate, pictures were used in wall paintings and windows to depict stories from the Bible. Portraits were not attempted but symbols, emblems and attributes were used which could be instantly identified. Above the west door of the south chapel is an Agnus Dei, the Lamb of

Maltese Cross and Cross Fouchée (above) and two masons' marks(?) (below) carved on the outside of the church

Agnus Dei and dragon carved on the outside of the church

God. When John the Baptist saw his cousin Jesus coming to be baptised he said, 'Behold the Lamb of God, which taketh away the sin of the world'. The Lamb, with one foot raised carrying the Banner of Victory, was a symbol used for Jesus and is still readily recognised. High up above the traces of the north porch can be seen Dextra Dei—the right hand of God, signifying entry into the Divine Presence. In a corresponding position on the interior wall of the nave is another Dextra Dei enclosed in a cross with heart-shaped spaces between the arms. It has recently been suggested that could be the head of the cross which once stood on the common opposite Cross Cottage and was broken during the Reformation.

On the buttress of the south chapel is a sundial which has been reused in some phase of rebuilding. Such sundials, or Mass dials, were semicircular in shape and marked off into eight, three-hour segments by lines radiating from the centre of the straight line at the top. In the centre a pin or rod, known as a gnomon or indicator, was set to cast a shadow on the dial and indicate the time. The lines for 6am, 9am, noon, 3pm and 6pm were marked at the lower ends with a cross, and shorter lines in between marked periods of 1½ hours. Originally the Garway dial would have been set somewhere readily seen on the south side of the church, facing south to catch the sun, now it faces west and although of no use anymore provides a good example of its kind. A similar dial in the church at Kirkdale, North Yorkshire has been dated to 1055–1066.[21]

References

1. A detailed description of the running of the Knights' hospitals is given in Jonathan Riley-Smith's book *The Knights of St. John in Jerusalem and Cyprus*.
2. *The Knights of Malta*, Joseph Attard.
3. In his historical introduction to the Rev. Larking's Report of Prior Philip de Thame 1338, John Mitchell Kemble suggests that the name *camera* derives from the room in which the estate's accounts were recorded before being despatched to Clerkenwell. The word originally meant a vaulted room, but came to mean a small estate.
4. *Rural England*, edited by Joan Thirsk.
5. Kemble gives details in *The Knights Hospitallers in England*, edited by Rev. Lambert B. Larking.
6. Described by D.W. Whitfield in *Medieval History* Issue 4, 'It was common practice for religious houses to acquire further financial income by appropriating the endowments of certain parish churches'.
7. *A History of the Order of St. John of Jerusalem in Wales and the Welsh Border*, William Rees.
8. These calculations have been made with the help of a Herefordshire baker and the Wye Valley Brewery.
9. Given-Wilson, Chris and Macdougall, Simone, *An Illustrated History of Medieval England*.
10. RCHM *Herefordshire*, Vol III & 'St. Giles' Chapel, Hereford' by Alfred Watkins, *Trans. of the Woolhope Naturalists' Field Club,* 1927.
11. *Water Mills of the Monnow & Trothy*, 1978.
12. *Evidence on Welsh Beekeeping in the Past*, Eva Crane & Penelope Walker.
13. C.W. Perkins, in an article for *American Historical Review* XV.
14. In 1930 the Rev. E. Hermitage Day wrote an historical pamphlet *The Preceptory of the Knights Hospitallers at Dinmore* for the library of the Hospital of St. John's Gate. In it he explains what happened to Garway immediately after the Dissolution of the Monasteries, a telling example of the struggle the Hospitallers had before they could claim the Templar lands they had inherited.
15. George Marshall, *Trans. of the Woolhope Naturalists' Field Club* 1927.
16. *An Introduction to English Church Architecture* Part 2, Francis Bond.
17. *Antiquaries Journal* Vol. VIII, April 1928.
18. In their book *The Crusades*, Louise and Jonathan Riley-Smith give details of two bulls of Pope Innocent III in which he calls for funds for the Fourth Crusade.
19. George Marshall, *Trans. of the Woolhope Naturalists' Field Club* 1927.
20. Pevsner, *The Buildings of England, Herefordshire*.
21. Hunter Blair, P., *An Introduction to Anglo-Saxon England*.

Index